Sondheim and
Into the Woods

'The Woods are just Trees. The Trees are just Wood.'

Stephen Sondheim and James Lapine combined fairy tales including Little Red Riding Hood, Cinderella, and Jack and the Beanstalk to create *Into the Woods* (1987). Funny and heartfelt, this musical explores what it might mean to act responsibly in society, both as a parent and as a child.

Situating the work within Sondheim's oeuvre and the Broadway canon, Olaf Jubin first offers a detailed reading of the show itself, before discussing key productions in New York and London, and 2014's Oscar-nominated screen adaptation. The radically different approaches to staging *Into the Woods* are testament to how open the musical is to re-interpretation for new audiences.

A combination of critical interpretation with performance and film analysis, as well as an overview of popular and critical reception, this book is meant for anyone who has enjoyed *Into the Woods*, be it as a musical theatre fan, an enchanted audience member, a student or a dedicated theatre professional.

Olaf Jubin is Reader in Media Studies and Musical Theatre at Regent's University London, and has written and edited several books on the mass media, popular culture and musical theatre.

The Fourth Wall

The Fourth Wall series is a growing collection of short books on famous plays. Its compact format perfectly suits the kind of fresh, engaging criticism that brings a play to life.

Each book in this series selects one play or musical as its subject and approaches it from an original angle, seeking to shed light on an old favourite or break new ground on a modern classic. These lively, digestible books are a must for anyone looking for new ideas on the major works of modern theatre.

Also available in this series:

Coming soon:

https://www.routledge.com/The-Fourth-Wall/book-series/4THW

Sondheim and Lapine's
Into the Woods

Olaf Jubin

Routledge
Taylor & Francis Group

LONDON AND NEW YORK

First edition published 2018
by Routledge
2 Park Square, Milton Park, Abingdon, Oxon, OX14 4RN

and by Routledge
711 Third Avenue, New York, NY 10017

Routledge is an imprint of the Taylor & Francis Group, an informa business

British Library Cataloguing-in-Publication Data
A catalogue record for this book is available from
the British Library

Library of Congress Cataloging-in-Publication Data
A catalog record for this title has been requested

ISBN: 978-1-138-29103-4 (pbk)
ISBN: 978-1-315-26569-8 (ebk)

Typeset in Bembo
by Apex CoVantage, LLC

For my mother, Helga Jubin, and the memory of my father, Bernhold Jubin.

Contents

Figures

Introduction *or* 'Once upon a time'

A fairy tale musical like no other

A rapping witch? Charming princes who woo not one, but several fair maidens? A Little Red Ridinghood ostentatiously displaying the wolf-stole she tailored out of the animal that previously devoured her? A Cinderella who isn't all that certain she actually wants to live in the palace? An enchanted forest where the good characters are just as likely to be rewarded as they are of losing all they hold dear? A fairy tale that does not end with 'Happily Ever After', but with a plea for considering others and an affirmation of community values?

Clearly, *Into the Woods*, the second collaboration of composer–lyricist Stephen Sondheim and librettist–director James Lapine after 1984's Pulitzer Prize-winning *Sunday in the Park with George*, is not your typical family musical based on the fairy tale stories by the Brothers Grimm or Charles Perrault. In fact, this multi-layered work could not be further removed from the Disney (or DreamWorks) screen-to-stage transfers – like *Beauty and the Beast* (1994), *Shrek* (2008) and *Aladdin* (2014) – that followed it. Where they offer straightforward, simple narratives with the heroic protagonists and hiss-worthy villains firmly in their established place, *Into the*

Woods (ITW) takes a revisionist approach to traditional fairy tales. Neither its densely plotted libretto nor its gorgeous score settle for the occasional post-modern joke, but enter new territory with a complex re-evaluation of those stories that is as witty as it is moving. Not content to be merely hip, cool or beguiling, here is a family musical that explores what pursuing your dreams and realizing your wishes really means, for the individual as well as for her/his community. People may enter these woods at their own peril, to be surprised and enriched by the wonders in store. So let the journey begin to find out what beckons when one ventures *Into the Woods*, a show that since its premiere 30 years ago has become one of the key musicals of the Broadway canon.

The genesis of *ITW* is well documented. In November 1985 there was an informal presentation of the show's first draft and of the main musical motifs, which was followed in June 1986 by a second reading of the material. At that time the plot was finalized, and Sondheim had finished all the songs of Act One. A few months later, in the autumn of 1986, there was a workshop at Playwrights Horizons, with a subsequent tryout at the Old Globe Theatre in San Diego. The musical premiered on Broadway on 5 November 1987, where it ran for 764 performances and won three Tony Awards for 'Best Score', 'Best Book' and 'Best Actress in a Musical' (Joanna Gleason). It became one of the few Sondheim shows to turn a profit, and a subsequent touring production around the United States also did very well at the box-office.

ITW represents Stephen Sondheim at his very best: the score is both melodious and full of humour, containing many of the artist's most accessible songs from the hilarious comedy of 'Agony' to the wistful 'No More' and the achingly beautiful 'No One Is Alone'. The show imbues its centuries-old fairy tale archetypes with complex personalities that turn them into utterly unique three-dimensional protagonists. With the possible exception of *Sweeney Todd, the Demon Barber of Fleet Street* (1979), especially admired and therefore regularly staged in London, *ITW* is undoubtedly Sondheim's most popular and widely known musical. Its school edition (omitting the darker Act II) is regularly performed all over the US, acquainting many a stage-struck young performer (and their parents) with the work of the greatest living musical theatre songwriter.

The show can be seen as another of Sondheim's playful inversions of musical theatre tradition, here, that of the American fairy tale musical as established by close Sondheim associates Rodgers & Hammerstein (*Cinderella*; 1957) and Mary Rodgers (*Once upon a Mattress*; 1959). While the first of these is firmly in the mould of the earlier Broadway classics by the same authors (such as *Oklahoma!*, 1943 and *The King and I*, 1951), resulting in an adaptation that is as sincerely romantic as it is calculatedly charming, the latter aims to counteract the familiarity of its plot by filling it with decidedly quirky characters and droll humour. Thus the two musicals can be said to have established the basic modes of fairy tale retellings still dominating the Great White Way even today: there is just as clear a link from *Cinderella* to *Beauty and the Beast* and *The Little Mermaid* (2008) as there is from *Once upon a Mattress* to *Shrek* and *Aladdin*.

In contrast to these models, the UK has a completely different tradition of fairy tales on stage, mostly due to the continued popularity of pantomime. All around Britain, productions of this genre constitute a ritual family outing at Christmas time and treat their source material with a knowing wink of irreverence that is far more lowbrow than any Broadway entertainment. The standardized story-telling and staging techniques of pantomime invariably include cross-dressing in the form of the pantomime Dame and the Principal Boy, saucy jokes and a continuous breaking of the fourth wall, including audience participation. (For more on the genre and its place in British theatre, see Taylor 2009).

ITW on the other hand opts for a decidedly postmodern approach to the subgenre of the fairy tale musical that proved utterly unique. This may have been because it was deliberately ignored by more recent examples of the form including the works of Disney Theatrical Productions, which were content to present the tales they are based on in a more traditional way, the occasional self-referential joke notwithstanding.

It is fairly ironic that *ITW* was later filmed by Disney, as the Sondheim–Lapine musical carefully eschews many of the regular tropes to be found in that movie company's classic retellings of fairy tales: there are no cute sidekicks, the story-telling although brisk is rather intricate, the running time exceeds two-and-a-half hours and the stage show is not afraid to include the occasionally disturbing violence that marks the original tales by Charles Perrault and the Brothers Grimm.

Nevertheless, there are also close links between the musicalized Disney versions and the Sondheim–Lapine collaboration. The opening number 'Into the Woods', already leaves no doubt that Sondheim's score was inspired by the kind of ditties that can be found, for instance, in those classic Disney cartoons released between 1937 (*Snow White and the Seven Dwarfs*) and 1981 (*The Fox and the Hound*). It is important to keep in mind here that *ITW* was written before the beginning of the so-called Disney Renaissance, which started in 1989 with *The Little Mermaid*, two years after the Sondheim musical opened in New York. The songs used in the Disney cartoon musicals that were released from the 1990s onwards are often longer and far more elaborate than the musical numbers in films such as *Pinocchio* (1940), *Cinderella* (1950), *The Lady and the Tramp* (1955) or *Sleeping Beauty* (1959). To give but one example from each of these four films: 'Give a Little Whistle' (1:35 min.), 'Bibbidi-Bobbidi-Boo' (1:17 min.), 'The Siamese Cat Song' (2:08 min.) and 'I Wonder' (1:32) are all much shorter than the average musical theatre song. But as so often with Sondheim, the composer and his librettist take the familiar – in this case, the fairy tale-based musical – and then turn it inside out to reveal unexpected layers and give them new relevance.

In *ITW*, Sondheim and Lapine aim to look beyond the surface of classic fairy tales by combining several well-known stories into a new plot. In this context, the two artists employ a rather unusual story-telling technique that mixes the age-old structure of the folk tales with decidedly modern elements: the stories practically move in circles, as their usual strictly linear development is affected whenever they overlap. Whereas in other theatrical works, a logical dramaturgy drives the plot, here it is the stereotypical behaviour of fairy tale characters who do not always act rationally since they are at the mercy of all-consuming desires that over-ride sensible action and that infuse the show with exactly the kind of archaic quality avoided in the musical's storyline (Spohr et al. 1994: 747).

In order to allow a new perspective on the overly familiar folk tales and to sound out the psychological depths of their heroes, heroines and villains, both the libretto and the score make explicit references to the symbolism of both Sigmund Freud and Carl Jung. Furthermore, the highly idiosyncratic approach of Sondheim and Lapine is obvious in the rather astonishing fact that the only real love song in the whole show ('I Guess This Is Goodbye') is performed by Jack, when he expresses his feelings for Milky White, his favourite pet (Banfield 1994: 395).

One of the key themes of the musical is the relationship between parents and children; both generations have to learn during the piece that growing up and being an adult is less about fulfilling your dreams than it is about accepting moral responsibility. That the group of fairy tale characters can only survive when the outside danger (i.e. the wife of the giant) is tackled collectively and everybody not only contributes but also shows consideration for the others, marks *ITW* as a rather unusual addition to the Sondheim canon: 'The cynicism, isolation, and alienation implicit in other works is tempered with an unfamiliar plea for commitment and communal awareness. The naïveté of youth is transformed into a sober acceptance of reality' (Gordon 1990: 308). Since the early 1970s, Sondheim's shows have explored the idea that compromises – in one's personal and artistic life – are inevitable, no matter how much one might try to avoid them. *ITW* is typical of this theme. Even in the fairy tale musical, the individual and his/her desires have to be modified for, and sometimes subordinated to, the general good of the community.

I

'You're back again only different than before'

The show's place in Sondheim's oeuvre

While on first sight radically different from the Sondheim shows that preceded and followed it (*Sunday in the Park with George*; 1984, and *Assassins*; 1990), *Into the Woods* is nonetheless highly typical of the artist who is customarily credited with ushering in the concept musical. Once again taking full advantage of Sondheim's unmatched ability to extend character through song, *ITW* explores the necessity of making decisions and the difficulty of living with their consequences (see *Company*, 1970, and *Follies*, 1971) while insisting that – to quote John Donne – 'No man is an island'. The actions of the individual inevitably have implications for those around him/her, highlighting (as in *Pacific Overtures*, 1976; *Assassins*, 1990, and *Road Show*, 2008) that the personal is always political.

In *ITW*, Sondheim's melodies have simple structures and don't exceed a length of 8, 16 or – at the most – 32 bars. The whole score is founded upon three basic musical ideas: the rhythmic 'journey' motif (made up of quarter notes), the 'magic beans' motif (a melody consisting of five notes) and the chord that accompanies the witch's spells (Banfield 1994: 393).

The composer explained that he modelled his songs to suit the clearly-drawn fairy tale protagonists: 'I was primarily responding to the color of the characters. They're primary-colored characters and primary-colored music is called for' (cited in Banfield 1994: 390). The result is a show and characters whose simplicity and vivacity was unmatched in any previous Sondheim show. Helpful in this respect was the songwriter's self-professed talent for writing within a predetermined style: 'I'm a pasticheur. [. . .] I can imitate virtually any style of music after hearing it briefly' (cited in Hirsch 1989: 75). The composer aimed once again to seamlessly integrate dialogue and musical numbers, and as a consequence some songs are only performed in excerpts: 'There were some numbers that built to a climax, like "Agony", but for the others I wrote complete songs and then snipped them away into fragments and blended them in' (cited in Zadan 1989: 341). Orchestrator Jonathan Tunick explains that those short rhythmic and melodic fragments, which are carefully fitted in and which are partially reprised, imbue the score with a feeling of one continuous composition (Mankin 1988: 62). As a result, the texture of *ITW* resembles that of a through-composed work, since the show for long stretches eschews the customary alternation of dialogue and numbers, thereby broadening the scope of traditional Broadway entertainment. A testament to the close collaboration of book writer and song writer, the libretto interweaves spoken and sung word in a carefully devised montage that creates a world where characters do not start to sing only when their emotions are too strong to be expressed in dialogue, as they do in the classical book musical à la Rodgers and Hammerstein. Here, song is just as much a means of expression as talk is. This novel approach would be taken even further, in Sondheim and Lapine's next collaboration, *Passion* (1994), a musical that did not even list individual numbers in its playbill and may even be categorized as a tone poem.

Throughout his oeuvre, Sondheim rarely makes use of one of the main staples of Broadway song types, the love duet. This kind of ballad is often one of the highlights of traditional musicals, and that is also true for fairy tale musicals, with examples ranging from *Cinderella*'s 'Ten Minutes Ago' and *Once upon a Mattress*' 'In a Little While' to *Aladdin*'s 'A Whole New World' or *Frozen*'s 'Love Is an Open Door'. But in Sondheim's world the protagonists only rarely achieve the kind of unison that would make the disappearance of all emotional and intellectual barriers – which is implied by the intuitive deployment and joint singing of the same words and notes – plausible. It is rather telling that *ITW* has only one duet for the traditional couple – the Baker and his wife – in 'It Takes Two', yet includes two duets for the pompous, self-centred princes, 'Agony' and its reprise in Act II. This musical clearly is not concerned with the ups and downs of traditional romance, but rather uses its duets to demonstrate the costs of selfish acts and competitive behaviour and how they must be overcome to create a harmonious living space where everyone can survive and thrive.

As with all Sondheim shows, the initial reaction to *ITW* was decidedly mixed. Many people were surprised and even irritated by the songwriter's choice of source material. Fairy tales are known and beloved for their stereotypical simplicity and customary happy endings, and Sondheim is an artist with a clear inclination towards stories whose prevailing mood is bleak and which feature primal emotions. As he himself once admitted: 'I love to write in dark colors about gut feelings' (cited in Savran 1988: 225).

At first glance, the disturbingly sad, at times nearly morbid, literary fairy tales by Hans Christian Andersen seem far better suited to Sondheim's sensibility than the folk tale collections of the Brothers Grimm and Charles Perrault. But it is precisely the fact that the composer and his collaborator Lapine highlight and amplify the harsh and violent elements of these classic fairy stories that makes their musical so startlingly original: as a reminder of the darkness that hovers beneath even the happiest of endings – the 'ever after' – they show us the fragility of both individual contentment and a peaceful society. Sondheim and Lapine also indicate that both come at a cost and are intricately linked.

Act II, which sees events turn progressively more tenebrous and deadly, proved especially controversial and was often rejected by both reviewers and audiences. Martin Gottfried complained that the libretto runs out of ideas and loses momentum in the second half, which is not compensated for or obscured by the demise of several characters and an ending full of priggish homilies (Gottfried 1993: 180). In addition, Meryle Secrest questions why the Baker's Wife has to die halfway through the second act, especially since this means that the authors rid themselves of one of their most believable characters (Secrest 1998: 356). There were also opposing views regarding the quality of Sondheim's score: while Stephen Banfield praises *ITW* as Sondheim's most mature and impressive achievement up to that point (Banfield 1994: 382), Michael Walsh denigrates the songs as 'lesser Sondheim' (Walsh 1989: 215).

The songwriter has underlined repeatedly that for him the drama of his work lies within the characters, which explains why nearly all of his protagonists are torn, insecure and undecided. As an expressive means and a way of colouring his characters, both his music and his lyrics represent this internal conflict and insecurity. Although Sondheim's lyrics never lose their conversational tone once it is established early on in the show, the (self-)doubts and conflicting impulses of the cast of characters in a Sondheim musical are revealed in the following stylistic devices: 'throwaway lines, parenthetical statements, cut-off lines, hesitations and ellipses, irregular lengths, varying metrical pattern' (Cartmell 1983: 33–34). The indecisiveness of the protagonists and their often futile attempts to solve or even address their problems are also expressed musically: 'Sondheim's melodies avoid the clarity of progression: they swerve, advance, float, circle back like the very plots which they sing' (Young 2000: 83). In this respect, *ITW* proves the exception to the rule as its fairy tale characters show remarkable clarity of purpose and vision at the beginning of the show, only to lose that certainty once the consequences of their actions become noticeable. The confident 'can do' attitude of especially the younger characters displayed in Act I (the adults are more likely to question their own behaviour, but quickly convince themselves that a certain ruthlessness is both apt and justified) gives way in the second half to moments of (self-)doubt, apprehension and guilt.

2

'There are rights and wrongs and in-betweens'
Selfish aims giving way to considerate cooperation

The following five sections will explore how *Into the Woods* sets up its narrative, unfolds its plotline and develops its characters in the sequence in which they occur in the show as a helpful way to highlight how the musical introduces its themes and to illustrate how they generate meaning as well as depth throughout the piece. Sondheim and Lapine's work shows that:

- dreams, desire and happiness are not static, but are constantly being re-defined
- all members of a community are intricately linked
- society can only thrive/survive if the impulse to self-centeredness and competitiveness gives way to consideration and cooperation
- in the often volatile relationship between parents and children, the best intentions may lead to consequences that are both unexpected and unwanted
- every gain in experience involves a loss of innocence
- growing up means learning how to see beyond one's own wishes and feelings and accepting responsibility

- the true meaning of learning includes the realization that there are no moral certainties in life, but that all our ethics and values need to be questioned occasionally
- (fairy) stories help us to explore, to explain and to deal with the world around us.

These ideas emerge bit by bit; they unfold in stages, accruing meaning as well as becoming enriched in the context of the events described and interpreted below.

'One midnight gone': starting on the quest

Like every traditional fairy tale, *ITW* begins with the words 'Once upon a time' (p. 3). For adults, these words evoke early childhood memories of being read to by parents and other guardians, while for younger theatregoers this immediately signals the start of a fantastic tale of magic and adventure.

That opening line, though, is immediately followed by 'I wish' (p. 3), signalling to the audience that Sondheim and Lapine will shift the focus away from the quickly developing plot of fairy stories towards the motivation that propels their events forward: the ardent yearning of the protagonists ('More than anything . . .', 'More than life . . .'; p. 3) for something outside their reach, be it excitement, wealth or emotional support.

The musical does not waste any time. With the help of a narrator who is positioned 'outside' the stories at the side of the stage, it sets ups the parallel narratives of three famous fairy tale characters whose adventures can be told in bold strokes because their stories are utterly familiar: Cinderella who wants to attend the king's ball, Jack who is forced to sell his beloved cow and Little Red Ridinghood, on her way to bring wine and bread to her sick grandmother. Sondheim and Lapine's conception of the first song as a 'Prologue', however, is a clear indication that the musical will not be content merely to retell these popular tales, but that something else will dominate the proceedings.

The show's opening number runs to nearly 13 minutes as it needs to introduce the setting, various subplots, and 10 characters (not counting the Narrator), which it accomplishes with admirable efficiency. The sequence not only establishes the background of the three young protagonists, but also introduces a fourth story line of the Baker and his wife, a fairy tale invented by the two writers. These two characters, following the reductive story-telling style of tales passed down orally from generation to generation, never acquire first names but are identified solely by their profession or function in the story-telling. The couple longs for a child and that longing and their increasingly desperate and callous attempts to get what they want will interfere with the fates of everyone else in fairytale land.

Little Red Ridinghood, visiting the Baker's shop to buy bread for her granny as well as to secure sweets for herself, an initial sign of her self-centredness, is the first to announce that she is ready to venture into the forest, the place where adventure beckons and danger lurks. The girl exhibits the heartless pragmatism of children who have not yet understood the consequences of certain events when she ponders the fate of her grandmother: 'For all that I know, she's already dead' (p. 10).

It's important to keep in mind here that the fairy tales collected by the Brothers Grimm, Charles Perrault and others circulated at a time when the great forests of Europe were still wild, preventing easy navigation on one's journey through nature. For thousands of years the woods held a fascination for anyone having to find a path through or around them – a fascination that could easily turn to dread if one lost the way.

Of course, psychoanalytical readings of fairy tales by Bruno Bettelheim and Carl Jung have revealed that the tall, dark trees in these stories, never bare, can be interpreted as projections of the unconscious, the places in our minds and hearts, where our hidden, not yet acknowledged desires and fears are to be found. To step into that place affords the opportunity to become aware of and to acknowledge those desires as well as to confront and to conquer those fears. Sondheim and Lapine take this as their starting point for a revisionist post-modern reading of the stories that uses their primal appeal to explore their continuing relevance for all our lives, whether we are children or parents. And what better means to investigate moral behaviour than stories that famously always end with a moral, a lesson learned by the protagonist and one to be heeded by the listener?

The absurdities of fairy tales, where anything is possible, are driven home by the Narrator when he announces that the Baker's father presumably 'died in a baking accident' (p. 12) and by the matter-of-fact announcement of the Baker's Wife that they are being visited by 'the witch from next door' (p. 12). As is her wont, the Witch, being the traditional antagonist, sets further wheels in motion when she informs the Baker of a curse she placed on his family to render it childless. For reasons of her own, she now gives the couple the opportunity to reverse that curse should they bring her four items, an unusual number since most fairy tales invoke the numbers three or seven: a slipper as pure as gold, a cape as red as blood, a cow as white as milk and hair as yellow as corn, with the latter linking the events to yet another famous story, the one of Rapunzel in her tower. As in all fairy tales, this offer comes with an expiry date – the couple has three days before the opportunity is lost.

Explaining how the curse got placed, the Witch not only reveals the Baker's father to have been a thief, but also a rapist; that accusation can easily be missed in the fast-flowing rap cadences used in this section of the opening number, but it is a stark reminder of the often disturbingly violent events in fairy tales as well as a harbinger of the turn towards death and despair that will occur in the second half of the show. The shockingly selfish actions of the Baker's parents resulted in their daughter Rapunzel being taken away by the Witch and are mirrored by Jack's Mother who declares 'We have to live/I don't care how' (p. 15). Even Cinderella deliberates whether moral behaviour has any value when it is never rewarded: 'What's the good of being good/If everyone is blind/Always leaving you behind' (p. 11).

With all of the characters thus far introduced now shown to be highly motivated to leave their homes and discover whatever they are looking for in the forest, the number ends with the whole company delivering a final stanza of the rollicking title song that reduces their tasks and their aims to infinitives ('To see–/To sell–/To get–/To bring–/To make–/To lift–/To go to the Festival–!'; p. 21). At this point, the narrative drive is all about taking action, without any consideration of the consequences and costs these actions may have.

In the woods, we first follow Cinderella to her mother's grave where we learn that she has no specific desires apart from her wish to go to the ball. This will later explain her indecisiveness about what to do at the festivities when faced with a courtship she hadn't counted on. Next, a new character, the Mysterious Man, plants the idea in Jack's head that to exchange his cow for some beans may be rewarding, before we witness the famous first encounter of the Big Bad Wolf and Little Red Ridinghood.

The authors in this scene emphasize the sexual undertones of the original fairy tale, similar to Neil Jordan's 1984 movie *The Company of Wolves*, itself based on Angela Carter's revisionist retelling of the Perrault original. In asides to the audience, the predator shamelessly admits his lascivious desire to attack the grandmother and devour the little girl, thus making us his accomplices in the devious scheme, a masterful plan that we only dare to enjoy because we already know how the story will play out and because Sondheim here is at the height of his command in the writing of suggestive yet highly amusing lyrics. The Wolf's ravenous hunger – and carnal appetite – combine with his persuasive cunning in leading the girl astray from the right path/the path of righteousness to present a master class of seduction. This number ends with one of the funniest lines in the musical, revealing the kinky pleasure the Wolf gets out of his deception: 'There's no possible way/To describe what you feel/When you're talking to your meal!' (p. 26)

When the Baker and his wife encounter Jack, they realize that they cannot afford to buy his cow, and so, with the wife leading the way, they resort to tricking him into exchanging the animal for five of what they claim to be magical beans, not knowing that their deliberate lie is actually the truth. After the boy's tearful goodbye to his best friend, the Baker confronts his wife about her ruse; she defends her taking advantage of a simple-minded, trusting teenager by pointing out that 'Everyone tells tiny lies – /What's important really is the size' (p. 30). The punning final line of the song ('If the end is right/It justifies/The beans!'; p. 31) exposes not only

Figure 2.1 Some pathfinders cannot be trusted: Danielle Ferland (Little Red Ridinghood) and Robert Westenberg (the Wolf) in the original Broadway production, Martin Beck Theatre 1987. Photograph by John Persson, Courtesy of Photofest.

a surprisingly ruthless streak but also a moral relativism that will come back to haunt her and everybody else in the magic kingdom. Her behaviour would register as even more disturbing if the audience wasn't familiar with the rest of Jack's story: we can excuse the deceit because we know that at this moment it is necessary for the fairy tale to continue and will ultimately lead to a happy ending. It turns out that the Baker does not (yet) have the heart to follow her advice as his attempt to steal Little Red's cape from her is thwarted by the girl's cunning exhibition of woe (screaming and hysterical weeping), which makes him repent his action immediately.

The song 'Our Little World' was added for the first London production in 1990 to allow the audience insight into the relationship between the Witch and her ward by showing what kind of loving interaction the Witch is so desperate to preserve at all costs. This duet exposes her as an overanxious parent ('Children are a blessing/If you know where they are'; Sondheim 2011: 67), whose solution to any potential danger her child may face is to keep her locked up where she is always under her mother's control. With the very title of the song already hinting at the sort of artificial idyll that will not last, the girl is content at this point in the story with a secluded life which she deems 'perfect' (Sondheim 2011: 67), even though – or perhaps exactly because – it mainly consists of a narcissistic preoccupation with herself: 'Brushing my hair, combing my hair. Only my mother and me and my hair . . .' (Sondheim 2011: 68). Whatever minor irritations she has experienced, such as her mother's drooling, seem at first to be not significant enough to seriously affect her unnatural state of bliss. But then halfway through the song, after hinting that her own understanding of what constitutes a happy life is largely shaped by her mother's definition ('Our little world is perfect/Or at least so she says'; Sondheim 2011: 68) Rapunzel starts to list all of the little details that irk her about her guardian. This implies potential conflict and also suggests that what the Witch has been afraid of all along, has already happened, namely that her daughter Rapunzel has grown up to the point where she will no longer be able to disregard her mother's imperfections and will search for satisfaction elsewhere. But for now, the Witch is unaware of this and insists that the self-serving nature of their 'delicious' intimate togetherness will remain 'exclusive' and 'unchanging' (Sondheim 2011: 68), a delusion that will be shattered shortly afterwards.

While Rapunzel's Prince – another character only known by his 'profession' – learns about the beautiful girl hidden away in a door-less tower and proceeds to investigate the matter, the wolf succeeds in overpowering Little Red Ridinghood. The image of the wolf devouring the girl metaphorically suggests rape. Yet the Baker saves Granny and child, freeing them from the beast's stomach. With Granny persuading their saviour to take savage revenge ('. . . let the animal die a painful, agonizing, hideous death'; p. 34), the stage is set for the first of several musical numbers in which the characters sum up their adventures in songs that directly address the audience and provide a moral to their stories. In 'I Know Things Now', Little Red reveals that she has learned her lesson – that new experiences may be thrilling, but that they often include an element of danger, which ironically may add to the excitement. The newfound wisdom that your fellow creatures may be deceitful and that danger lurks where your parents do not want you to go is acquired alongside the realization that growing up and forging your own path inevitably results in a loss of innocence. Just as every child has to learn that 'nice is different than good' (p. 35), it will sooner or later recognize that learning more about the world means also learning more about its snares and one's own vulnerability, which in turn makes one value a child's state of ignorance.

Out of gratitude, the girl is finally ready to part with her hood, so the Baker now has two items from the list, but his newfound satisfaction ('feeling braver and more satisfied that he had ever felt'; p. 36) is immediately contrasted with Jack, who is chastised by his mother for giving away his cow for a mere five beans. By linking the events this way, the libretto underlines that everybody's actions impact on the lives of those around them and that egotistical behaviour is bound to harm others.

Next, Cinderella literally stumbles upon the Baker's Wife, who is intrigued to learn about the other woman's encounter with royalty. As with so many maidens in fairyland, she is fascinated by the Prince, his reported good looks and gallant manners; perhaps even by the dream of upward social mobility that is part of all Cinderella tales. The kitchen maid in the ball gown, though, is clearly ambivalent, feeling both out of place and out of her depth at the royal court. Only when the girl rushes off back home to her evil stepmother and stepsisters, does the Baker's Wife realize that Cinderella wears the golden slipper she is looking for; in the ensuing confusion, she accidentally loses the cow.

The first midnight has passed and the company steps out one after the other to sum up in short epigrams what they have learned and other pieces of information, including the Witch's 'Sometimes the things you most wish for are not to be touched' (p. 40), which will prove of importance later on, when it is revealed that she cannot have touched any of the items she has sent the Baker and his wife to retrieve.

'Two midnights gone': continuing the quest

Scene 3 begins with Jack whose song 'Giants in the Sky' tells us what happened once he arrived above the clouds; in contrast to Little Red he has not found a new world within, but outside the kingdom. While mounting the beanstalk, he gained a new perspective, reflecting the way that travel enables one to realize that one's own environment represents only a miniscule part of the whole planet. It is another law of relativity: looking back or – in this case – down '[i]s enough to show you just how small you are' (p. 42a). Freed from the usual family connections and seemingly freed from social constraints, Jack makes the mistake of assuming that he is also no longer bound by moral obligations ('You're free to do/ Whatever pleases you'; p. 43). Above the clouds, he is taken care of by a friendly female giant, who provides comfort in the form of food and affection, with the lyrics ('And she draws you close/To her giant breast'; p. 43), once again hinting at a sexual experience. This suggestion would explain the violent reaction of the male giant who threatens to kill Jack, a threat that makes the boy re-evaluate his regular life, which may not be exciting, but at least is safe ('. . . it's then that you miss/All the things you've known'; p. 43). Grabbing whatever valuables he can ('You steal what you can and run'; p. 43), Jack descends back to earth, realizing that neither extreme is what he wants in the future. His home has been revealed to him as small and limited, whereas the kingdom in the sky may offer riches, but also hides mortal dangers. Therefore, a compromise between the two ('And you wish that you could live in-between . . .'; p. 44) now appears the most tempting option. Yet the experience has changed Jack forever. He can never forget his discovery that there is so much more than the finite part of the world he assumed was all there is. He ends the song with the same excited announcement he had made at the beginning to anyone who will listen, that there is a whole new life (form) out there, at once awe-inspiring, frightening and marvellous: 'There are big tall terrible awesome scary wonderful/ Giants in the sky' (p. 44).

Jack's enthusiasm is dampened when the Baker refuses to sell him back Milky White and the new owner's vague promise that he might be tempted to part with her for more money, induces the boy to risk another climb up the beanstalk. The Baker's unwillingness to be honest about Jack's chances of getting back his friend, plants seeds of something just as dangerous as the beanstalk – false hope and the reckless behaviour that inevitably goes along with it.

Next follows 'Agony', the duet of Cinderella's and Rapunzel's Princes, one of the highlights of every production of *ITW* and one of the songs that regularly receives the most applause. These two brothers meet by chance in the woods and confess to each other the trials and tribulations of winning their respective damsel in distress. Astounded by the fact that anyone would want to run from the future king, Cinderella's Prince begins by admitting that part of the maiden's attractiveness is her unattainability – the fact that 'the one thing you want is the only thing out of your reach' (p. 47) makes her the perfect object of his desire. Rapunzel's Prince counters with the claim that the girl he himself is infatuated with is causing him an even bigger headache, revealing a competitive trait matched by his brother. Their one-upmanship with regard to who must face the more daunting tasks reveals these traditional fairy tale heroes as vainglorious lugheads who in spite of their splendid appearance and glorious singing voices prove that (masculine) beauty can be just as misleading an indicator of character as it is with Cinderella's evil stepsisters. 'Agony' ends with the Princes' vow to prevail and to marry their respective beloveds, but the song as a whole makes the audience wonder whether Cinderella's Prince can really be the solution to all her problems and whether he is actually worthy of her.

One person who hasn't yet recognized that the two 'sensitive, clever/Well-mannered, considerate,/Passionate, charming' (p. 48) heirs to a throne are attractive only on the surface is the Baker's Wife; her fascination with nobility leads her to the follow Rapunzel's Prince to the beauty locked up in a tower and thus to the third item, the hair as yellow as corn. She rips out a strand of it with only the slightest of regrets and soon has a chance to retrieve the last ingredient demanded by the witch, Cinderella's golden slipper, as the latter has once again run away from the King's festival into the woods in order to lose her pursuing Prince. Just as her husband had done in his earlier encounter with Little Red Ridinghood, the Baker's Wife tries to take away the item she needs by force, and like him she fails, 'embarrassed by her own behaviour' (p. 52). The audience perceives that the couple is only resorting to desperate means because their values have been momentarily corrupted by the promise of fulfilling a desire too strong to resist. They are not bad people, but in the breathless anticipation of finally being granted what they have always wished for, their moral compass is no longer reliable – like so many of the characters, they are lost in the woods.

While part of the Princes' allure for the Baker's Wife is their chivalrous comportment, tellingly she staunchly rejects attempts by her husband to behave in a similar manner when trying to reverse the curse placed on his family. This indicates how we often do not recognize or value in the people closest to us certain traits we admire in strangers. She repeatedly ignores the Baker's commands to exit the woods and to leave the task of finding the magic objects to him, partly because they do not appear as gallant, but as dictatorial and chauvinistic. That he is less level-headed, more forgetful and more scrupulous than she is, reinforces her argument that he will not be able to fulfil the Witch's demands on his own. Once he acknowledges this, after she has shown him Rapunzel's hair, they take stock of their journey up to this point in the song 'It Takes Two', the first number in the show to emphasize that certain goals can only be reached by joint efforts and by pooling resources. To their own amazement, the Bakers find that each of them has developed, manifesting qualities they were unaware of and did not even suspect existed; in the process of establishing a real partnership, they have realized some of their so-far untapped potential. The Baker may originally have been convinced that 'one was enough' (p. 54), but he now sees the errors of his way. He needs his wife, just as she needs him, because 'what needs to be done/You can do/When there's two of you.' (p. 55). This assertion of shared responsibility and joint endeavour will, in Act CII, be expanded beyond the couple as the smallest example of a group to the larger assembly of the whole community. The musical carefully moves from the achievements of the single protagonist to those of pairs and then larger groups, along the way demonstrating how in any society all individuals are intricately linked.

But just when the Baker and his wife begin to look optimistically towards the future, Milky Way keels over and dies; as the Witch reminds everyone, two midnights have gone, signalling that the couple has only one day left to find a replacement. In their desperation they take another cow and cover her in flour, a strategy that fools no one. In any case, it turns out that the cow's death can easily be reversed by the Witch's powers. Here Sondheim and Lapine over-complicate their plot. As with the revelation late in the first act that the hair as yellow as corn is not Rapunzel's (since the

Witch has touched that particular ingredient) but can simply be replaced with hair from a corn cob, this development not only adds another unnecessary complication to a first half that is very long anyway – Act I runs to about 105 minutes – but it also defies the internal logic of fairy tales in which a task is set and then achieved, by substituting trick alternatives at the last minute. (It would be as if the Prince, having searched the kingdom for Cinderella by insisting that every woman tries on her slipper, were then to identify her by accidentally discovering her ball gown in her wardrobe.) Basically, Sondheim and Lapine set up a new fairy tale (of the Baker and his wife) and then do not follow the rules of the genre. This seems inconsistent because the other fairy tales incorporated into *ITW* still do.

'It's nearing midnight': completing the quest

Time running out, however, is not the only problem the Witch has. She has learned of the Prince's visits to Rapunzel and is outraged that the girl has ignored her warnings not to interact with anyone else, least of all with handsome strangers. Insisting that as a parent she knows best ('Why could you not obey/Children should listen'; p. 59) the Witch is fully aware of how attractive the world outside the tower must seem for Rapunzel, and she attributes her own inadequacy as sole companion to her ugliness, suggesting why she is so keen on regaining her beauty. She resignedly reminds her ward of all the dangers that could befall her once she leaves the only place that the Witch can completely control. Fairy tale characters both good (princes) and bad (wolves) can be found out there, but the list tellingly culminates in the most unpredictable and unreliable of creatures: 'humans'

(p. 60). As most parents, the Witch is anxious to shield her daughter from disappointments and hurt, yet her only strategy is to insist that the girl should '[s]tay a child while you can stay a child' (p. 60), wilfully ignoring the fact that there comes a time in every child's life when parents are no longer sufficient because of the adolescent's exploratory drives (including a budding sexuality). The Witch penalizes Rapunzel by cutting off her hair, a clear symbol of her femininity and sexual attractiveness, forcing her back into the state of gender-neutral childhood, and then abandoning her in the desert, before attacking and blinding her suitor. But all these measures come too late; once Rapunzel has had her first taste of freedom, no punishment will keep the girl in her place. Like most draconian sanctions, the Witch's drastic actions only further alienate the child from the parent.

Experience has also changed Little Red Ridinghood; having skinned the Wolf herself and now parading a beautiful wolf-skin cape, she is no longer unprepared for potential attacks but carries a knife; conversing with Jack, she dares him to go back up the beanstalk to steal the Giant's golden harp. The competitiveness of the two young characters resembles that between the two Princes and already prepares the audience for the ending, when the two will become siblings in a blended family.

The third day in the woods also marks Cinderella's third and final visit to the ball, but although she has once again managed to escape the Prince, this time she leaves something behind: one of her slippers gets stuck in the pitch on the castle stairs. In 'On the Steps of the Palace' Cinderella makes us privy to the internal dialectical process by means of which she weighs one alternative possibility against another, without being entirely satisfied with either. Although his tenacity impresses her, the Prince's continuous attempts to keep her in the castle only exacerbate her own inability to choose what she desires. She is afraid that the Prince has a false impression of who she is – not entirely unfounded considering that she attended the ball in what amounts to a disguise – and that a life as the Princess is not actually what she wants for herself because she feels out of place among royalty. Thus, the daunting task of having to make a momentous choice that will affect her whole life is simply too much at this point. So, instead she arrives at the conclusion that it is best to postpone her own decision, thereby placing the responsibility for whether or not a relationship will ensue on the Prince. By deliberately leaving him her slipper as a clue, she avoids making a choice – something that will become impossible in the second act.

Now hobbling around in just one shoe Cinderella refuses the offer by the Baker's Wife to exchange the slipper for the last remaining magic bean, which she carelessly tosses into the underwood, completely unaware of possible consequences. Yet she consents to the suggestion of taking the shoes of the other woman, which will allow her to run away faster from her prince, and so the Baker's Wife obtains the final item just in time for midnight.

Before the Witch can go to work to reverse the curse, Jack's Mother informs everyone that a dead giant lies in her garden, a piece of news whose significance nobody recognizes yet, partly because all the other characters selfishly assume it doesn't concern them, which is why they bluntly refuse to help. The Witch resurrects Milky White, and once the cow has been (force-)fed the remaining ingredients (including the hair from the corn cob), she gives milk for the first time. After drinking the potion, the Witch regains her former beauty, a transformation that unfortunately results in the loss of her powers.

In this musical every gain is accompanied by a loss, just as all experience is accompanied by a forfeiture of innocence, optimism or trust. In like manner, the Mysterious Man is revealed to be the Baker's father who ran away from his responsibilities, afraid to face the consequences of his thoughtless acts; having supported his son and daughter-in-law's efforts to lift the curse, he dies as soon as the task is accomplished. With the telling of two classic fairy tales already completed, the final scene of Act I shows us how the Prince finds his Cinderella, not sugar-coating the brutal yet unsuccessful attempts of her evil Stepmother to present each of her two daughters as the proper owner of the slipper by cutting off their heel and toes, respectively. This represents another extreme measure by a parent to secure what is presumed best for their offspring, even if it involves physical harm.

The Narrator fills us in about what has happened to Rapunzel in the interim. Having borne twins, an illogical detail, because, as part of the Baker's family, she, like her brother, should have been unable to conceive, her tears restore her Prince's eyesight, so everything is set for a better future. While the good characters are rewarded, the bad ones – like the evil stepsisters – are taken to task by Cinderella's animal friends, the birds, which pick out their eyes, a cruel punishment that will be restaged on a larger scale in the second half. With everyone appearing to receive their just deserts, the company is ready to sum up their experiences for us in the Act I finale, 'Ever After'. The 'villains' (stepsisters Florinda and Lucinda as well as the Witch) resignedly admit that they were mistaken in their greedy pursuit of the unattainable, because there are certain imperfections that we all must learn to live with: 'Had we used our common sense/ Been worthy of our discontents . . .' (p. 77), they would not have risked losing their eyesight and what made them special.

Yet, the rest of the company takes a stand in favour of setting individual goals and venturing out into the unknown: 'When you see your wish, pursue./It's a dangerous endeavour,/But the only thing to do . . .' (p. 77). The song then leads back to a reprise of the opening number 'Into the Woods', bringing us full circle. But just before the characters can sing '. . . happy ever after!', the traditional last words of every fairy tale that are always heavily laden with meaning, the Narrator manages to interject, 'To be continued . . .' (p. 78), while we see a second giant beanstalk growing up to the sky.

'It's the last midnight': finding the culprit

Considering that all the various stories appear to have reached a positive conclusion, the question arises of how the plot can be continued. Haven't the tales ended as they were supposed to end? Haven't the good characters been rewarded and the bad ones been punished? Just as in Sondheim and Lapine's first collaboration, *Sunday in the Park with George* (1984), both audiences and reviewers initially criticized the second act of *ITW* repeatedly, arguing that the first half – like *Sunday*'s – constitutes a perfectly realized show that did not require another act, especially in view of the fact that Act II of *ITW* incorporates a major shift of tone towards a darkness that many theatregoers could not handle, rendering the show unsuitable for very young children. In musical theatre it is extremely rare to find material aimed at children given a dark twist that may even make adults uncomfortable; the only other comparable example might be the unsettling

grotesquerie of *Shockheaded Peter* (1998). That work transformed the often sadistic cautionary tales of Heinrich Hoff-
mann's controversial children's book *Struwwelpeter* (1845)
into a series of vignettes that all end with the death of a child
and thus embrace a narrative bleakness most Broadway or
West End shows avoid.

All other American musicals based on fairy tales, from *Once
upon a Mattress*, to the various versions of *Cinderella* or the Disney shows (like *Beauty and the Beast*, *The Little Mermaid* or *Aladdin*) are careful to remain family-friendly. They may include
the odd joke that intentionally goes above the head of a child,
but they refrain from lingering on scenes of death or present-
ing moral dilemmas that do not fall within the simplified fairy
tale dichotomy of either absolutely good or irredeemably bad.
While the first half of *ITW* can stand on its own, as attested by
the Junior Edition for performance by schools, its second half
adds several layers of significance to the material and shows
how much adults can still learn from fairy tales. At first glance,
Act II begins with lyrics identical to the opening of Act I,
suggesting the archetypal nature of all fairy tales, whether traditional, literary or rewritten. But the redecorated setting leaves
no doubt as to how much has changed for the protagonists,
because every change in living circumstances leads directly to
a change in desires. This may include the urge to act on new
responsibilities, to satisfy basic physical needs or to come to
terms emotionally with one's discoveries: enthroned in the
castle, Cinderella now wants to give a festival herself; the Baker
and his wife bemoan the lack of space in their home, now that
they have a son; while Jack misses the astounding world he
encountered at the top of the beanstalk. The Narrator assures
the audience that despite these various longings, the protagonists are 'content' (p. 85) – although he may intentionally

avoid the word 'happy', this is how the characters themselves describe their new lives (p. 85). Yet, they have already learned that the fulfilment of one fervent desire does not automatically render everything perfect: 'Wishes may bring problems,/Such that you regret them./Better that, though,/Than to never get them' (p. 86).

Just when the company is for the umpteenth time about to pronounce its current state of bliss, the fairyland is hit by what seems to be an earthquake, reducing the Baker's house to rubble and cutting off the lyric 'happy' at 'hap-' (p. 88). The shock and concern of the characters is supposed to extend to the audience; the stage directions read, 'We should be momentarily uncertain as to whether there has truly been an accident onstage' (p. 88). Whereas the fairy tale figures are puzzled by the destruction of their environment, the audience will be startled by Sondheim and Lapine's audacious suggestion that tales of human desire are not over when the protagonist has finally got what s/he craved for. The authors reveal the moral of fairy tales for what it is – an illusion. The belief that once one has amassed riches, married the Prince or defeated the villain all needs cease and all longing evaporates is a pretence. These are stories we tell children to render the world less frightening and their constant craving for more – be it food, excitement or attention – less impossible to fulfil.

The musical thus moves from individual problems to a catastrophe that affects everyone living in the kingdom, a threat that cannot be overcome by the heroic (or devious) deeds of one person alone. Together with the Witch, whose beautiful garden has also been devastated, the Baker and his wife conclude via a process of logical deduction that the destruction has been caused by another giant. Remarking that 'A giant's just like us – only bigger!' (p. 90), the Witch not only prepares us for the surprising discovery, that the creature is driven by the exact same motives – hurt, anger, thirst for revenge – as humans, but also hints at the fact that those we perceive to be 'villains' have feelings, too; a fact we all too easily and conveniently blot out. This point is taken up again later in the show when the Witch counters Little Red's justification that killing a wolf is not the same as killing a human being with the retort: 'Ask a wolf's mother!' (p. 107).

Seeking help from his neighbours, the Baker has to realize that he is now in a similar predicament to Jack's Mother at the end of Act I, with only a handful of his fellow fairy-land inhabitants – like Jack or Cinderella – even interested in his plight. Jack is prevented from coming to the Baker's aid by his mother, who responds to Jack's affirmation that his adventures have made him a man with the truism that in her eyes he will always be 'a little boy' (p. 92). Cinderella, on the other hand, trusts that her stout-hearted husband is the perfect person to confront and defeat the threat to his kingdom.

At first, the adults try to protect the younger characters from the truth in a well-meant, but ultimately futile attempt to shield them from the acute danger and the prevailing mood of hopelessness, not challenging Little Red Riding-hood's assumption that a 'big wind' (p. 92) blew down her home and killed her mother, a tragedy that she only later will fully comprehend. So the protagonists once more set out into the woods, this time in search of shelter and help or to attack the Giant.

Yet, even the forest has been affected. No longer majes-tic and mysteriously beautiful, the stage directions indicate that it is now just as chaotic and mirthless as the rest of the land: 'Something is wrong. The natural order has been broken. Trees have fallen. The birds no longer chirp' (p. 95). Next, a distraught Rapunzel accuses the Witch of ruining her chances of happiness; the Witch's attempt to justify her extreme actions – 'I was just trying to be a good mother.' (p. 95) – is very funny, partly because the audience can perceive the rationale behind this statement while recognizing the irony that in the misguided endeavour to shield her child from every evil, the mother has herself committed a number of crimes against her. Parents in the audience will be especially aware that they themselves are likely to have erred in similar ways; the painful truth is that the best intentions often lead guardians to adopt the most questionable of tactics and to cause more harm than good.

Also searching through the woods are the two Princes, but any hopes the other characters may have that these strapping rulers of the land will charge against the Giant are quickly dashed, as the debonair duo turn out to limit their heroic deeds to the perpetual wooing and defence of maidens. They are less inclined to aid any of their other subjects. Recognizing a fellow philanderer when they see one, Cinderella's and Rapunzel's Princes confide in each other in a reprise of 'Agony' that their eyes and minds have strayed – both are enamoured by two new damsels in distress who turn out to be Snow White and Sleeping Beauty. Again, each tries to outdo the other when describing the obstacles in the way of winning the hearts (and bodies) of these girls, comically revealing unexpected sensitivity (like squeamishness at the sight of blood) and peculiar neuroses ('Dwarfs are very upsetting'; p. 98). What makes this second version of the song so poignant is the realization that even a fairy tale prince is a creature of habit, who, unable to resist whenever he encounters a specific set of stimuli, is moreover conditioned always to react in an identical manner. Incapable of both fidelity and real leadership, they are exposed as the fairy tale equivalent of a Don Juan or a Casanova – hardly 'perfect husband' material.

With whatever pathways there once existed through the forest no longer recognizable, the Baker and his wife encourage Little Red to 'stray from the path', thus admitting that the rules taught to us in childhood are not timeless admonitions never to be questioned, but that there may come a time when those regulations are no longer applicable.

Together with the Witch and the former inhabitants of the castle including the Steward, one of the Prince's servants, and the rest of Cinderella's family, the characters chance upon the Giant who not only turns out to be female, but reveals that the havoc she has wreaked is in retaliation for her husband's death at the hands of Jack. This ingenious twist reminds us that even supposed 'monsters' have recognizable motives and feelings. Her demand to give up Jack so that she can punish him and her promise that she will then cease any further destruction, puts the inhabitants of fairytale land into a moral dilemma that they are incapable of resolving. The Witch has no qualms about handing Jack over to the Giant, which undoubtedly would result in his violent death, but as the boy is not present, her pragmatism leads to her considering several other characters as replacements. However, neither the Steward nor the blind stepsisters are willing to sacrifice themselves for the greater good. As so often happens when seeking a scapegoat, the group finally settles on an outsider, in this case, the Narrator. His claim that every story needs 'an objective observer' (p. 102) to pass it on falls on deaf ears, as it becomes clear that the other characters are all too willing to dispense with his services, not least because they 'don't like the way [he has] been telling' (p. 102) their story. In order to save his hide, the Narrator asks them to consider his unique position, which ensures that the plot will not become chaotic, because he alone knows how it should proceed. While this argument makes the Baker and his wife hesitate, the Witch grabs him and pretends to the Giant that he is the person responsible for her husband's deadly fall. Although the Giant immediately realizes that the Narrator is not Jack, he does not survive when she carelessly lets him drop from a great height.

With the demise of the Narrator, which could be seen as Sondheim and Lapine's cheeky musical theatre version of Roland Barthes' death of the author, the show not only enters the territory of post-modern story-telling, but also effectively announces to the audience, that from this point onwards, all bets are off, including the presumption that all fairy tales must end happily. As the Narrator points out himself, in the misplaced hope that it will save his life, only he of all the characters in the show knows the proper ending to the fairy tales presented here, so his murder leads to uncertainty. How will the various subplots resolve and will they resolve in the way we are accustomed to? With the death of the omniscient storyteller, the spectators lose the narrative link between their world and that of the fairy tale protagonists. There is no longer an intermediary and without his reassuring as well as distancing presence the audience becomes more directly involved with the events on stage. It is put in the same position as the characters: now *all* are at the mercy of (narrative) forces that are not even visible and thus are firmly outside their control. The disorientation and moral confusion of the people in fairyland becomes *our* disorientation, which makes their moral decisions easier to relate to and easier to evaluate.

Yet, the offering was in vain, as the Giant continues to demand Jack's rendition. Jack's Mother enters and tries to argue with the grieving widow by pointing out that her son had his own problems; her defiant words anger the female giant and when Jack's Mother threatens her, the Steward accidentally kills the older woman when he knocks her over the head to shut her up. Once more, understandable emotions – the fear of provoking a mighty force – acted on rashly, have led to inadvertent tragedy, the death of a person. In their desperation to get rid of the Giant, the company finally lie to her about Jack's whereabouts, pretending that he hides in the steeple tower.

But even this small falsehood has unforeseen, horrible consequences, because while making her way to the tower, the Giant tramples Rapunzel to death. A mourning Witch laments the tragic fate of her beloved daughter who failed to heed her mother when she warned her about the mortal dangers awaiting outside the tower in which she was kept prisoner: 'Couldn't you stay content,/Safe behind walls,/As I/ Could not?' (p. 105). Yet, Rapunzel only did what her mother did before her – move beyond the limits originally set by *her* parents. Thus the Witch's 'Lament' speaks for all those parents who have to stand by helplessly and watch their children being harmed, in spite of having been warned, which apparently supports the conclusion that 'Children refuse/To learn' (p. 106). The number concludes with the sobering insight that 'Children can only grow/From something you love/To something you lose' (p. 106).

In order to find Jack before the Witch does, the Baker and his wife separate and search different parts of the forest. This occasions another chance encounter between Cinderella's Prince and the Baker's Wife. It should be pointed out here that the way certain characters in the woods continuously stumble upon one another while others never meet, questions the whole concept of coincidence and suggests that in the woods we only chance upon what we are unconsciously looking for. Whereas the Baker never crosses the path of either of the Princes and in the first act only encounters those characters who may help him to undo the curse placed on his family (Jack, Little Red Ridinghood and the Mysterious Man), his wife walks directly into those people who can satisfy her long-standing curiosity about the Royals – first Cinderella and then the Prince himself. Just as the latter holds no fascination for the Baker or Jack, the Mysterious Man is of no real importance to the Baker's Wife or Cinderella, which is why they never bump into each other.

The Prince not altogether correctly identifies the Baker's Wife as a damsel in distress or at least as a person in peril and immediately turns on the charm to offer her princely protection in the form of physical closeness. His rapid switch into seduction mode at first catches the Baker's Wife by surprise since she is well aware that the good-looking hero's affections are usually reserved for a different sort of maiden: 'This is ridiculous,/What am I doing here?/I'm in the wrong story' (p. 109). Her self-awareness playfully reminds audiences of Sondheim and Lapine's ploy of mixing up several fairy tales. Nevertheless, the Prince eventually overcomes her objection that as both of them are married, it would be wrong to give in to their mutual attraction. He argues that with a giant on the loose, their lives may end 'Any Moment' and that the forest constitutes a realm where moral obligations cease to matter and where anyone could and should follow his or her deepest desires. After all, why not cherish one small moment of bliss in the face of mortal danger? So they act on their feelings and consummate their passion there and then.

The audience, though, is immediately made aware of the consequences this brief moment between a Prince and his subject will have, as after this incident their significant others meet and decide to join forces. The Baker thoughtlessly voices the popular opinion that a Prince's main occupation is to seduce 'young maidens' (p. 110), not realizing that at the same moment the heir to the throne is making love to his own spouse. Cinderella angrily insists that her husband is different, but the audience knows better and is thus prepared for the couple's separation later in the act.

Like all moments, the one between the Prince and the Baker's Wife passes quickly; no longer letting their emotions dominate their actions, common sense returns. Having fulfilled his duty of granting support, which the Prince misinterprets as offering her his body and his sexual prowess, he speaks a few perfunctory phrases before rushing off to his task of investigating the Giant, while the perplexed Baker's Wife is left to ponder how to make sense of her experience. At first, to preserve her self-image as well as her adulation of the man she has just slept with, she insists that he acted completely *in* character while she acted completely *out* of it: 'Was that him? Yes, it was./Was that me? No, it wasn't' (p. 112). The Baker's Wife has fallen for the Prince's public image and now refuses to confront her nagging suspicion that the behaviour of the real Prince is that of a conceited playboy rather than that of the fairy tale hero, whom she has admired from afar and dreamed of for years.

How to reconcile what has just happened with the rest of her life, with her duties as wife and mother? What seemed possible in the woods – to enjoy the romantic attentions of a handsome prince – is inconceivable in her mundane day-to-day existence, but doubts have set in and continue to linger ('Why not both'; p. 112). So why should she content herself with a marriage that provides emotional support ('warmth'; p. 112) and financial stability ('bread'; p. 112), but lacks sexual excitement? That the Baker's Wife does not dare to put her frustrated physical desire into words – the Prince's allure is coyly summed up as 'whatever' (p. 112) – but rather tries to obscure what exactly made the royal such an attractive alternative, suggests that certain needs are so difficult to admit that we prefer not to articulate them clearly.

Now that she has had a taste of what she has been missing so far, the Baker's Wife struggles to return to her regular life where the fulfilment of some of her desires is not even a possibility. Once you have made certain choices, i.e. once you have committed yourself, your options are limited, a fact that the Baker's Wife resents: 'Is it always "or"?/Is it never "and"?' (p. 112). But then thinking the matter through, she arrives at the insight that on the one hand, the woods are not a place where you can actually live, which means in the context of reading the forest as the unconscious, that most of our existence needs to be controlled by *conscious* decisions and desires. On the other hand, a life where every urge is satisfied and every dream comes true, would make it impossible to cherish those occasions when one has achieved what one has hoped and worked for: 'But if life were only moments,/Then you'd never know you had one' (p. 112). Therefore it is preferable not to obsess over lost opportunities that may never come again or chances that may never arrive, but instead to value that special moment, however fleeting, because it gives additional meaning to the choices you have to make later in life.

The Baker's Wife has hardly finished putting her insight into lyrics when she is accidentally killed by the Giant, while she rampages through the woods. This plot development is more than just startling; it is actually one of the most

problematic aspects of the whole show. First of all, the Baker's Wife is one of the most intriguing characters in the musical, so her death leaves an unsatisfying vacuum at the heart
of the proceedings. Even more disturbing for the audience is
the fact that her death seems unwarranted. So far, only minor
characters have died. We do not care very much for either
Rapunzel or Jack's Mother, but to kill off the Baker's Wife
immediately after she has cheated on her husband, seems an
unduly harsh punishment for a moral lapse that has no comparable consequences for the male protagonists. Sondheim
and Lapine may have intended her death as a jolt to increase
the stakes and make audiences realize that nothing is off limits
and that nobody is ever entirely safe, but it appears to express
an overly moralistic statement along the lines that wives who
stray will have to endure horrid repercussions.

When the Baker learns of his wife's passing, he is just as
stunned as the audience. But the Witch as unsentimental and
pragmatic as ever, confronts him with the harsh realities: 'Wake
up! People are dying all around you. You're not the only one
to suffer a loss. When you're dead, you're dead' (p. 114).
Since the Witch has apprehended Jack, the discussion once
again reverts to whether or not he should be handed over to
the Giant. Now personally affected by the crisis, the grieving
Baker accuses the boy of being the one to blame for his own
and everybody else's tragedies. This triggers a heated argument
in song – 'Your Fault' – in which the Baker, Jack, Cinderella,
the Witch and Little Red Ridinghood try to determine who
exactly is answerable for what has happened, pointing fingers
at all the others while defending their own selfish actions. The
blame gets shifted to and fro several times, before the Witch,
tired of everybody else's unwillingness to accept responsibility
for their egotistical behaviour, readily steps up one last time

to claim her role as everybody's villainess, singing her show-stopping exit number 'Last Midnight': 'Placing the blame,/ If that's the aim,/Give me the blame –/' (p. 121).

As Bernadette Peters, who was the first to play the part of the Witch on Broadway, so memorably put it, the character basically reads her fellow fairyland citizens 'the riot act' (quoted in Anon. 2002[c]: 23). She chastises the other four protagonists for their flawed ethics that allow them to act recklessly while still pretending to themselves that they have not done anything wrong ('You're not good, You're not bad, You're just nice'; p. 121); she despairs over a seemingly unbreakable cycle of generations of morally compromised characters who will always put their selfish interests first: 'You're all liars and thieves,/Like his father,/Like his son will be, too –/Oh, why bother?'/You'll just do what you do' (p. 121). Maybe because she has lost her own daughter and because all of her attempts to save the kingdom have been thwarted, the Witch throws around magic beans, no longer caring what the consequences might be, but instead now actively seeking the punishment that earlier in the show she had striven to reverse, anything to part with a society that disgusts her: 'All right, Mother, when?/Lost the beans again! Punish me the way you did then!/Give me claws and a hunch,/Just away from this bunch' (p. 122). In a final spectacular demonstration of fairy tale magic and theatrical illusion she disappears into the ground.

'That's what woods are for': the process of learning

The Witch's outburst has sobered up the other characters who are finally ready to admit their own mistakes to themselves and to each other. The Baker, however, has still not come to terms with suddenly being a single parent; he leaves his son with Cinderella and rushes off into the woods. Here, he meets the Mysterious Man again, who responds to the Baker's assertion: 'I thought you were dead' with a cheerful, 'Not completely. Are we ever?' (p. 123), revealing to the audience the idea that the influence of parents does not end with their demise, but that the values they have inculcated and the emotional bonds established with their children remain alive in their consciousness for decades to come.

The Mysterious Man confesses that he shirked his duties as a father out of ignorance, fear and guilt, alerting his son to the danger that he is about to make the same error because he is overwhelmed by events and can take 'No More'. Acknowledging that parents are fallible and that their influence on their offspring only ever diminishes to a small degree ('We disappoint,/We disappear,/We die but we don't . . .'; p. 123), the father draws his son's attention to the fact that children, who, in trying their utmost later in life not to repeat their parents' mistakes, are in their turn likely to be guilty of other mistakes. Nevertheless, recognition of their own shortcomings does not necessarily lead them to accept those of their mothers and fathers: 'They disappoint/In turn, I fear./Forgive, though, they won't . . .' (p. 123). But fear of failure should not lead to a refusal to engage at all, because as a parent (or in more general terms, as a member of society), a life of total isolation is impossible. The nagging suspicion that one may have failed one's children will only be replaced by other worries, for instance, how the children are coping without their father or mother and whether there was not something one might have done to improve their lives.

Every action has repercussions, especially in our dealings with children, but while that responsibility and the surprises life may spring upon us may at times be daunting, the temptation to run away has to be resisted. At the end of the song, the Baker accepts his part in the generational contract when he joins the Mysterious Man in the line: 'Like father, like son' (p. 124). He also realizes that in order for all of them to 'just pursue our lives/With our children and our wives' (p. 125), they will first have to conquer the Giant, and so his final 'No more' at the very end of the song, signals a new-found determination to actively fight the danger that engulfs the whole kingdom.

The Baker, Cinderella, Jack and Little Red hatch a plan to kill the Giant, which shows how they have learned from previous experiences as it involves trapping the Giant in pitch, blinding and then striking her. While they prepare the assault, Cinderella meets her husband, whom she confronts with her knowledge that he has betrayed her. The Prince tries to explain his philandering in the following words, 'I thought if you were mine that I would never wish for more. And part of me is content and as happy as I've ever been. But there remains a part of me that continually wants more' (p. 127). In the end, he blames his imperfections on the way he was brought up: 'I was raised to be charming, not sincere' (p. 127). This line always gets a big laugh, partly because its spontaneous candour is so striking, but also because it reveals that the Prince's education, which was intended to prepare him for life as a fairy tale hero, has transformed what should have been awe-inspiring character traits into compulsive behaviour patterns that render him unsuitable for precisely the sort of long-lasting relationship promised by fairy stories. With this Prince – and Rapunzel's – there is no 'happily ever after', since all he is good for are 'moments in the woods'. Husband and wife agree it is best for them to separate and in their final farewells admit that what they fell in love with was their own fantasy of each other, before that idealized image crumbled under the strain of everyday existence ('I shall always love the maiden who ran away'; 'And I the faraway Prince'; p. 128).

With the trap set, Cinderella reassures Little Red Ridinghood that attacking the Giant is a defensible plan, while the Baker consoles Jack who has just learned of his mother's death. The teenage girl objects that killing the Giant is extreme, because she is 'a person' (p. 128) and asks whether her mother's Christian insistence that people should always 'show forgiveness' (p. 128) no longer applies – a question that the musical never answers directly, preferring instead to let the actions that follow speak for themselves. The adults address the younger generation's concerns with one of Sondheim's most beautiful numbers, 'No One is Alone', a song that has been consistently misunderstood. Far from being an example of typical Broadway uplift such as 'You'll Never Walk Alone', the ballad is a moving invitation to accept that in spite of what our parents first teach us, life has no absolutes and that there comes a time when we will be forced to make our own decisions and can no longer rely on those closest to us to make them for us or to advise us: 'Mother cannot guide you./Now you're on your own./Only me beside you./Still, you're not alone./No one is alone, truly./[. . .]/You decide what's good./You decide alone./But no one is alone' (pp. 128–129). But without an unwavering guide we can look to for help, how can we make informed choices? How can we know how to react? When we feel uncertain ('Nothing's quite so clear now –'; p. 130) and confused ('Feel you've lost your way?'; p. 130), maybe it is best to remind ourselves that every individual has his/her own motives and that each of our actions and words will not only affect ourselves but other people as well – sometimes people we did not even have in mind: 'You move just a finger,/Say the slightest word,/Something's bound to linger,/Be heard' (p. 130).

Everyone makes the wrong decision once in a while, but perhaps it is easier to accept this and to forgive ourselves and others when we remember that what we have been told in our youth needs to be questioned at times: 'Witches can be right,/Giants can be good' (p. 131). Not everybody shares our point of view, our predispositions and our values, which is why we need to remember that there is always a different perspective, and whoever has chosen that alternative position is also not alone. Any interaction in society, be it between children and parents or between groups with opposing interests can only be successful when we show consideration for those whose affairs and well-being are intricately linked to ours. Yet 'No One Is Alone' must not be interpreted as sanctioning moral relativism as is implied near the end of the ballad in the lines 'Hard to see the light now./Just don't let it go' (p. 132) We need to hold on to those ethical convictions and codes that guide us, even if their power diminishes occasionally, since they still serve as a moral compass to point out the right direction in times of confusion.

In a joint effort of humans (both young and older) and birds, the female Giant is slain, thereby overcoming the danger. In the final moments of the show each of the characters, dead or alive, re-appears to offer us a moral. The Baker and Cinderella decide to move in together and take in the orphaned Jack and Little Red Ridinghood, forming a blended family that is held together just as much by affection as it is by necessity as they need each other's help, company and support. The Baker's last remaining doubts that he may be unsuited to raising children are put to rest by his wife who advises him to explain the baby's unusual living arrangements, including the loss of his mother, by telling their story. Devising tales – fairy tales and others – is how we learn about ourselves, about the past and the world we live in; it is what artists do as well as parents. That last refrain of 'No One Is Alone', featuring the Baker's Wife wasn't added until Broadway, and according to actress Joanna Gleason made all the difference in how the audience perceives the character, allowing them to connect to her more strongly as well as adding another level of poignancy to the show (Roberts 2002: 20).

It is left to the Witch to remind us of the responsibility that comes with telling those tales. In 'Children Will Listen' (p. 136), in clear opposition to her bitter announcement earlier that 'Children *won't* listen' (p. 106), she emphasizes that all our actions will be closely observed by those around us. Children look to us for moral guidance and though they may not always follow our instructions, the way we explain the world to them as well as the way we interact with others exerts an influence. This is why we need to be fully aware of the social rules and ethical values we impart as a means of navigating through life: 'Careful before you say,/"Listen to me."/Children will listen' (p. 136).

Substituting 'wishes' for 'children' in the second stanza, the song not only refers back to the story of the Baker and his wife, whose most fervent wish was to have a child, but also insists that to pursue any dream – or even simply to talk about it – may have long-lasting repercussions and may even involve some loss. This also applies to 'spells', or any other form of grievance, resentment or revenge, because no one can know what they may yield in the future: 'Sometimes the spell may last/Past what you can see/And turn against you . . .' (p. 136).

In the final three lines, the song comes full circle, with the Witch concluding: 'Careful the tale you tell./ *That* is the spell./Children will listen . . .' (p. 136). These lines hold multiple meanings: on the one hand, they refer to the fact that often our very words come back to haunt us, for instance when children point out inconsistencies in our behaviour ('But you said, one should never lie . . .') – a situation that undermines our authority and thus our standing in the eyes of those we wish to guide. On the other hand, children are trusting and because they love us and we have power over them they are enthralled by us; with this comes the added responsibility that we need to be careful how we instruct them. As any teacher sooner or later realizes, it is reckless to forget the duty one has to provide students with accurate information, as they will employ this knowledge in various ways in interacting with the rest of society.

The company next goes into one last reprise of the title song, with a few telling changes: when pursuing your dreams and dealing with difficult situations, it is pertinent to consider the wishes and ambitions of others ('You can't just act,/ You have to listen'; p. 137) and to take a moment to weigh all alternatives before making a choice ('You can't just act,/ You have to think'; p. 137). The world at large is a place that is sometimes perilous and often frightening, and the same can be said about the unconscious, because to confront one's deepest fears and longings is intimidating. But that does not mean one should retreat into one's shell since the rewards of roaming freely or of honest introspection are plentiful. Instead, each of us must take into consideration what brought her/him to this specific situation ('. . . mind the past'; p. 137) and ponder where one needs to go and what one's individual decisions may bring about ('. . . mind the future'; p. 137).

All of one's experiences, whether good or bad, increase the individual's understanding of self or others and this is what learning really means: '. . . everything you learn there/Will help when you return there' (p. 137).

Studying any subject, including studying oneself and society, entails periods of uncertainty and doubt: 'you have to grope,/But that's the way you learn to cope' (p. 138). While the process involves trial and error, knowledge accumulates and allows us to appreciate details and complexities: 'Into the woods, each time you go,/There's more to learn of what you know' (p. 138). Again emphasizing that labels such as 'dangerous' or 'enemy' should be questioned and not simply accepted at face value, the song now includes the lines: 'Into the woods/To mind the wolf,/To heed the witch,/To honor the giant' (p. 138) and replaces the self-serving and potentially careless actions of Act I ('To see −/To sell −/To get −/To bring −/To make −/To lift −/'; p. 21) with more considerate infinitives: 'To mind,/To heed,/To find,/To think,/To teach,/To join' (p. 138), which culminate in celebrating togetherness and sharing joy: 'To go to the Festival!' (p. 138). With this in mind, the musical can without reservations finally allow the prospect of things turning out well: 'Into the woods,/Then out of the woods −/And happy ever after!' (p. 138).

Before the curtain falls, though, Cinderella pipes up one last time with 'I wish . . .' (p. 138), avoiding the closure at the end of traditional fairy tales, instead hinting at a yet unfulfilled desire that might potentially motivate the continuation of her own and everyone else's story. This serves as a final reminder that happiness isn't a permanent state, but a fleeting condition because it is constantly redefined. What makes us human is our never-ending striving for improvement of our own situation and of society in general. In real life, the journey is never over, mostly because one's own path intersects with those of others. This, of course, is borne out by the musical itself: in spite of the fact that it tells several fairy tales at once, all of them are linked to one other because, contrary to what we may assume, our own destiny is bound to those around us, each person with their own desires and predicaments. In the end, life is one complicated story for all of us.

3

'Valuable things that I hadn't thought to explore'

Interpreting *Into the Woods* on stage

In order to chart the reception of the musical over the last 30 years, this fourth chapter will compare the most important productions of the fairy tale musical in both the US and the UK. It will not only discuss the different interpretations of the show, but also provide a brief overview of the critical response to the show itself and its various major incarnations.

Like all Sondheim musicals, *Into the Woods* has continuously attracted exceptionally talented performers, including Bernadette Peters, Joanna Gleason, Chip Zien (New York 1987), Julia McKenzie, Imelda Staunton, Ian Bartholomew (London 1990), Clare Burt, Sophie Thompson, Jenna Russell, Damien Lewis, Sheridan Smith (London 1998), Vanessa Williams, John McMartin, Laura Benanti (New York 2002), Hannah Waddingham, Helen Dallimore, Jenna Russell, Michael Xavier (London 2010), as well as Donna Murphy, Amy Adams, Denis O'Hare and Jessie Mueller (New York 2012), which to some degree has coloured the reactions of both audiences and reviewers.

As is customary with all of Sondheim's shows, his score (and to some degree Lapine's book) found a lot more favour

with critics when *ITW* was revived than in Lapine's first production, even though the first revivals themselves (2002 on
Broadway, 1998 in London) were regarded as less accomplished than the first production (Jubin 2005: 820–821). This
phenomenon can be observed with practically all of Sondheim's works and might best be described as a case of 'familiarity breeds admiration'. Because the composer never does
the expected, each new musical makes initial interpretation
and categorization difficult. His scores demand careful listen-
ing and, therefore, many of their intricacies are often only
discovered and subsequently appreciated when reviewers
have had time to explore them in more detail, for instance
with the help of a cast recording or repeated viewing. This
also applies to *ITW*, but with this show, it also seems to have
been the marked difference in tone between the two acts that
put off the first night critics.

The major difficulty with *ITW* is to find a consistency
of mood between the show's two halves as they have often
been criticized for being incompatible – what starts out as a
witty frolic involving occasionally questionable moral decisions turns into an increasingly bleak portrayal of physical
and emotional devastation. Fairy tales are conventionally
about lessons learned and good behaviour rewarded, and the
authors of *ITW* do not shy away from pointing out how
hard-won some wisdom is and how difficult it can be to
decide what constitutes 'good' behaviour in certain situations. As the above reading of the musical has shown, Sondheim and Lapine carefully prepare for the mayhem in Act II
on the one hand through foreshadowing and on the other
hand by the simple conceit of allowing their protagonists to
follow their obsessive behavioural patterns through to the
often bitter end. As a result, the audience recognizes that its

notions of determination, spirit of adventure, pluck, and success are relative when viewed in a wider context.

In the same way that the illustrations of a fairy tale book create a framework that determines how readers and listeners visualize the stories in their imagination, so do the set, costume and lighting design of any production of *ITW* play an important part in creating a stage world in which anything from transcendent magic to unexpected tragedy might be possible. If the musical is to cohere as a work where the second half logically and persuasively follows from the first, both silliness and death must be conceivable.

The original Broadway production garnered a lot of praise for its production values, which included costumes by Ann Hould-Ward, lighting by Richard Nelson and scenery by Tony Straiges whose sets took their cue from etchings of storybooks and so offered front-cloths of castles and cottages. This premier staging relied to a large degree on the scenography to underline the increasing darkness of the material. The stage showed thick, asymmetrical woods made up of twisted, silvery trees with bare branches as well as thorny thickets that became progressively overgrown; the lighting of these was at first sunny and later eerie. Nonetheless, few reviewers were convinced by the change of tone in Act II; after all, the production greeted the audience arriving before the show and returning to their seats during the interval with birdsong. Wrong-footed by the unexpected turn events take in Act II, the New York critics bemoaned what they perceived to be a preachy, didactic second half. Some members of the audience shared their dissatisfaction. Kim Crosby who played Cinderella, later remembered: 'In the second act you were undoing everyone's expectations. You could feel it in the air, especially when we started getting high school classes that got kind of restless. More than one time we found M&Ms on stage' (quoted in Anon. 2002[a]: 23).

Still, in spite of the mixed reviews, *ITW* turned out to be Sondheim's second longest-running show on Broadway with 764 performances, only topped by *A Funny Thing Happened on the Way to the Forum* (1962, 965 performances). The success of the first New York production may be partly attributed to its three Tony Awards and to the fact that in spite of its darker second act, the show is far more suitable as an outing for (older) children and thus as family entertainment than *Follies*, *Pacific Overtures*, *Sweeney Todd*, *Assassins* or *Passion* by the same artist, a public perception that certainly was supported by *ITW*'s beautiful, storybook-inspired sets and costumes. That the show opened at a time when there were hardly any child-friendly shows on Broadway apart from *Cats* (1981) may have also helped with ticket sales.

The first London staging in 1990 could not have been more different in design and tone; this was the British premiere of a Sondheim show that veered furthest from its original New York production. It also illustrates what can be gained by the writers' openness to different approaches to their material, an increasingly rare attitude in an era where practically all hit musicals from *The Phantom of the Opera* (1986) and *The Lion King* (1997) to *Mamma Mia!* (1999) and *Hamilton* (2015) are franchised as carbon copies of the premiere production. Directed by opera director Richard Jones and designed by his regular collaborator Richard Hudson, the artistic team of the 1990 *ITW* went for a surreal environment in the form of a nursery room with trap-doors in the floor, which was furnished with chairs with antlers for backs. The room had a curved wall with nine oak doors as well as hidden windows and was partly wall-papered with a forest, engraved in black and white. Here, the woods had already entered the supposedly safe home, alerting audiences that our desires and fears cannot be shut out once they have taken root. Later, as the kingdom and its society started to disintegrate, the wall of the room was demolished and the forest peeled away. In addition, the performers were often lit from below by old-fashioned footlights, not only creating sinister shadows but also throwing the characters literally into harsh contrast to their magical environment.

Thus, the picture-book prettiness of the 1987 Broadway original was refitted as a gothic nightmare seemingly inspired by the illustrator Gustave Doré. With the proceedings thus

Figure 3.1 A fairy tale world rendered ominous by set design and lighting – the cast of the first London production of *ITW*, Phoenix Theatre 1990. Photograph by Michael Le Poer Trench, Courtesy of ArenaPAL.

decidedly unsettling from the very start, the more violent developments of Act II did not come off as a stunt but rather seemed like a logical progression of events, set in a world where everything was off-kilter anyway. Even more than their New Yorker colleagues, however, the London reviewers on the whole objected to the dramaturgical developments after the interval, accusing the show's creators of, variously, pretentiousness, sentimentality or being too clever by half. In spite of the occasional glowing notice, this British production closed early after 197 performances, when it became a victim of the sharp decrease in theatre attendance following bomb threats against the West End, which were triggered by the 1991 Iraq war.

The first important revival of *ITW* was staged just eight years later, in London's tiny Donmar Warehouse, which seats only 251 and which after highly successful runs of *Assassins* (1992) and *Company* (1995), both directed by the venue's artistic director Sam Mendes, had earned a reputation for (re)discovering Sondheim musicals in small-scale productions. This time, the show was staged by John Crowley and designed by his brother Bob, whose ingenious set for the very limited stage space at the Donmar drew a lot of praise for its clever use of perspective. Bob Crowley would later design several musicals for Disney, including *Mary Poppins* (2004), *Tarzan* (2006, which he also directed) and *Aladdin* (2011), and so would move from a postmodern approach to children's stories to a far more straightforward rendering of family entertainment and fairy tales. Helped by mood-enhancing lighting designed by Paul Pyant, Crowley's designs for the Donmar *ITW* presented a background wilderness of fir trees with an illuminated miniature castle on top and employed a tiny revolve that transported the

characters seemingly inevitably into the forest. The 1998
revival proved that *ITW* is another Sondheim show that,
like *Sweeney Todd* for instance, works in all kinds of different
environments and may actually benefit from being presented
in a chamber version without lavish scenery, but with the
audience sitting very close to the proceedings.

While many critics deemed the production to be vocally
underpowered as only Clare Burt (the Witch), Sophie
Thompson (the Baker's Wife), Nick Holder (the Baker)
and Jenna Russell (Cinderella) seemed technically capable of

Figure 3.2 There is room for a forest in the smallest (stage) space:
the cast of the 1998 production of *ITW*, Donmar Warehouse 1998, including Clare Burt (on the far right) as
the Witch and Sophie Thompson (second from the
right) as the Baker's Wife. Photograph by Donald
Cooper, Courtesy of Photostage.

doing justice to Sondheim's demanding score, most of them agreed that Sheridan Smith as Little Red Ridinghood was an absolute find. The Donmar production completed its scheduled two month-run without transferring to a bigger West End Theatre. On the whole, the show received more praise for its book, lyrics and music than the first London staging at the beginning of the decade; it seems that in the intervening years, the British reviewers had caught up with the show and had learned to value its libretto and score.

When James Lapine returned to the show he had co-written in order to direct the first Broadway revival in 2002, he pushed the musical more towards traditional family entertainment. Lapine not only inserted another fairy tale – the three little pigs make a fleeting appearance, which means there is also a second wolf – but he cast both Little Red Ridinghood and Jack as pre-pubescent teenagers, thus adding figures of identification for young audience members as well as veiling the sexual connotations of their songs and scenes. The one change, however, that drew most of the attention was replacing Milky White, a wooden prop on wheels in 1987, with an actor (Chad Kimball) whose vaudevillian antics now drew most of the laughs. To many, the occasionally melancholy dancing cow seemed symptomatic of a directorial approach that aimed to downplay the harsher elements of the show in order to make it more family-friendly. Once again, the design elements, sets by Douglas Schmidt, costumes by Susan Hilferty and lighting by Brian McDevitt, went for enchantment and picturesque allure – similar to *Beauty and the Beast* – rather than for uneasiness and unsettling strangeness. The gigantic leather-bound fairy tale books with gold-lettering literally coming to life, ensured that the sets were pretty, but also quite conventional.

The press speculated that these revisions and the traditional design approach were partly a response to the increased presence of Disney on the New York stage, whose screen-to-stage transfers *Beauty and the Beast* (1994) and *The Lion King* (1997) had proved immensely popular. With its eyes on the lucrative family market, the revival also seemed to reflect the fact that *ITW* in the 15 years between its first and second Broadway production had become a staple of church, community and school productions, the latter usually performing a shortened version for children that omits the more violent Act II. Although the cast of 2002 on the whole was deemed inferior to the 1987 original, with Laura Benanti's Cinderella praised as the one stand-out performance, the revival ran for 279 performances. Its main significance is that it paved the way for the Disney film adaptation, which would arrive in cinemas more than a decade later and which maintained the new focus on the material first exhibited in 2002.

The 2010 Regent's Park Theatre production was the first major open air staging, and the fact that the show began during daylight and three hours later ended in the dark under the stars enriched one of the musical's most pertinent themes. Director Timothy Sheader commented:

> How appropriate that we start this journey into the woods in shared light. We arrive as single beings and as we travel deep into the night sky we become, however transitory, a community, listening, digesting and hopefully shifting in some small way.
>
> (Sheader 2010: 9)

Sheader's interpretation opened with a young English school boy walking onto the multiple-tier set by Soutra Gilmore

that skilfully combined the existing trees with artificial ones
and scaffolding. Carrying a sleeping bag and his rucksack,
he seemed to be replaying a recent argument with his father
('Get out of my sight!' – 'I hate you!') and the audience
could conclude that he may have run away from home. The
boy unpacked various toys (like old Barbie and Trolls dolls
and stuffed animals) and started the musical as our Narrator, displaying the enjoyment children get from mixing up
stories and often mischievously interacting with the various
fairy tales figures without them noticing it. For instance,
he pulled Florinda's hair for which Cinderella was slapped.
At the end of the first act, the boy went to sleep, assuring
his toys that the story is 'to be continued'. Act II opened
with ominous voices echoing through the woods and the
fairy tale characters now directly addressing the boy and fac-
ing dangers that he himself seemed to be afraid of – had he
unleashed more than he could handle? At the end the boy's
father (who figured in his story as the Baker, the man who
desperately wants a child) came to find him in the woods
and they embraced during 'No One Is Alone'. Prompted by
the Baker's Wife, the Father started to tell his son the story
to assure him that things were alright now, when the Witch
took over with 'Children Will Listen', indicating that the
Father may have been partly responsible for his son's running
way. The final 'I wish' was spoken by the boy to indicate
that his fantasy was uncurbed; clearly, he would continue
to make up stories. Director Timothy Sheader's framing
conceit of a young boy as the Narrator worked exceedingly
well especially later in the story, when the increasing violence visited upon the characters became an expression of an
angry child's casual cruelty as well as his fears, since the boy
was also frightened by his surroundings. (He was the one

to point out: 'There's something in the glade there'.) The production thus not only showed how we invent stories to come to terms with what has affected us, but also how the relationship between parents and children is often volatile, with both sides acting impetuously and rashly. But once we have had time to reflect – in the boy's case via acting out the impulses of violence and impatience through devising a fairy tale – we recognize that we may have been short-tempered as well as short-sighted and that the love that unites us is stronger and more important than what vexes us about the other generation.

Figure 3.3 An expert blend of existing nature and artificial forest: the cast of the 2010 London revival of *ITW*, on the multi-tiered set designed by Soutra Gilmore, Regent's Park Open Air Theatre 2010. Photograph by Catherine Ashmore, Courtesy of the photographer.

The Regent's Park revival was re-staged and partly re-designed for a star-studded outdoor production in Central Park in 2012, which was slightly less enthusiastically received by New York critics and whose planned transfer to a conventional Broadway theatre never materialized due to scheduling problems. Shortly afterwards, it was announced that more than 25 years after the curtain first came up on *ITW*, a film version of the stage musical was at last to hit cinemas.

4

'Nice is different than good'

Rob Marshall's 2014 movie adaptation

Into the Woods nearly made it onto the silver screen as early as 1997: Columbia Pictures was about to greenlight the project when a change in studio executives at the beginning of the year led the film company to put the project in turn-around. Lowell Ganz and Babaloo Mandel had written the screenplay for this adaptation, which went through roughly 30 drafts. An excerpt from their first version, dated 1992 and published in *The Sondheim Review* a decade later, reveals a handling of the material that with its mixture of jokiness and sentimentality is similar in style to other movies centring on family life (like *Parenthood*, 1989; *Father's Day*, 1997; or *Tooth Fairy*, 2010) written by the same team, but that appears too coarse and too flat-footed for the subtlety and intricacy of the original stage work. The unproduced screenplay opens with the lines: 'Once upon a time, there lived a Baker and his Wife. And they wanted a child . . .' (Anon. 2002[b]: 25), which already fails to successfully imitate the tone of classic fairy tales. The screenwriters then underline the quickly set up premise with a rather contrived first scene that shows the husband's misinterpretation of his spouse's joy at having removed a jelly stain from his apron (!) as a hint that she is finally pregnant.

By the time the film was shelved, Sondheim already had composed two new songs, a different opening ('I Wish') and another duet for the Baker and his wife called 'Rainbows'. The first number changes the approach to the narrative by introducing certain main characters (like Cinderella and Jack) strictly as part of a community where everybody wants something they feel is missing from their lives. This is explained to us in short lines given to various villagers; only later will we find out that a few of these people have greater importance for the plot than others. At the same time 'I Wish' firmly puts the childless couple centre stage (or rather centre screen) by repeatedly returning to their hope of one day having 'a pink and creamy/screamy/dreamy baby' (Sondheim 2011: 106). The second song contrasts the Baker's pessimism and willingness to settle for less with his wife's insistence that 'Love isn't enough/We need some dreams' (Sondheim 2011: 109). While neither song was included when the musical finally was adapted for the cinema in 2014, 'Rainbows' is nowadays often inserted into the Sondheim two-hander *Marry Me a Little* (1980).

Yet, the composer–lyricist did contribute one new song to the 2014 version, 'She'll Be Back', no doubt to allow the film to be able to be nominated for a 'Best Original Song' Academy Award. The song was intended for the moment when Rapunzel, reunited with her prince, leaves the Witch. The song begins with the first lines of 'Lament' (not used in the film since the girl does not die) and then shows the Witch trying – and failing – to convince herself that her daughter's declaration that she never wants to see the Witch again is not what she really meant. The sequence is beautifully lit by Dion Beebe, but as it only spells out what the viewer surmises anyway, it does not add anything new, but merely holds up the action, which is why it was decided to cut it from the release print. It is included, though, in the bonus material on the Blu-ray version of the film.

Rob Marshall has stated repeatedly that he first thought of adapting *ITW* for the screen when he watched US President Barack Obama address the nation on the 10th anniversary of 9/11 with the words 'You are not alone'. On the one hand, this anecdote later turned into a nice marketing ploy; on the other, the fact that Marshall immediately connected Obama's remark – which has a completely different meaning – to one of the musical's key songs, reveals that the Oscar-nominated director, like so many critics before him, has misunderstood the ballad.

Disney left nothing to chance, casting its screen version with considerable star power even in the smallest roles (Meryl Streep, Chris Pine, Anna Kendrick, Emily Blunt, Johnny Depp, James Corden, Tracy Ullman). The studio also took great care to keep the show's originators happily involved in the project: James Lapine was hired to adapt his own libretto and – as with Tim Burton's 2007 film version of *Sweeney Todd* – Stephen Sondheim was close at hand to suggest cuts and to discuss the changes necessary to secure a reasonable running time of 125 minutes. As a consequence, several songs were deleted, including 'I Bet This Is Goodbye', 'Maybe They're Really Magic', 'Ever After', 'Agony (Reprise)' and 'No More', with the latter used as underscoring when the Baker meets his father in a mystifying encounter near the end of the movie. It is easy to see why 'Ever After' and 'No More' were cut: the movie would have no interval and would feature voice-over narration by the Baker instead of a traditional Narrator, which is a rather un-filmic literary device. The removal of these and the other numbers may allow the plot to move along faster, but as a result certain characters lose some of their complexity. The Baker and his wife struggle less with their devious schemes to retrieve the required items, only Cinderella's Prince is unfaithful (and seemingly no more than once), and the Baker's understandable first impulse to run away from a situation that threatens to overwhelm him is now overcome in a quick dialogue exchange with his deceased father. On stage, the hilarious reprise of 'Agony' provides a welcome antidote to the mood of death and despair that permeates the second half of the musical, which in the film remains unrelieved.

Yet, whereas John Logan's adaption of Sondheim's 1979 musical thriller merely re-arranged *Sweeney Todd*'s major elements – less focus on the innocent lovers and the widespread corruption in Victorian society, and more emphasis on the deranged psyche of two doomed obsessives whose ghost-like appearance already hints at their inevitable demise – the simplifications and plot changes in Lapine's screenplay rob the movie of *ITW* of some of the show's most intriguing layers. It also relies too much on voice-over narration: the script takes the short cut of telling us things instead of dramatizing them.

In this case, streamlining the complicated events in the stage musical, which is roughly 160 minutes long, leads to characters who are less ambiguous and cunning: the Baker and his wife assume straight away that the beans must be magic ('These must be the Witch's beans'), so their exchange for Jack's cow seems less like taking advantage of a gullible victim. Cinderella has now lost both her mother and father

('the poor girl's parents had died'), to avoid any uncomfortable questions as to why her father doesn't stop the abuse
she suffers from the hands of her stepmother and stepsisters.
Instead of leaving it to his servants to diffuse the threat of
the Giant, while he scampers around the woods looking for
the next maiden to shield from harm, in the film Cinderella's Prince announces that he himself will investigate the
disturbance in his kingdom – a task he completely loses
sight off once he has hooked up with the Baker's Wife. The
encounter between the Prince and the Baker's Wife is shot
so discreetly that it leaves open the possibility of their never
having ventured beyond one kiss. We only see her put her
scarf back on.

Lapine's decision to reconceive Little Red Ridinghood
and Jack as children instead of teenagers, repeating the
approach of his 2002 Broadway revival, results in a loss of a
very important level of ambiguity. Not only does it remove
any sexual suggestiveness from the girl's encounters with
the Wolf, which leads to an oddly ineffective performance
of 'Hello Little Girl' by Johnny Depp, but the question of
whether or not to deliver Jack to the Giant becomes much
less complicated as for most moviegoers the sacrifice of a child
would be unimaginable. The number of deaths is reduced to
three (Jack's Mother, Granny and the Baker's Wife). Unfortunately, due to the decision to spare Rapunzel and the Narrator, here replaced by a voice-over of the Baker, the fatal
accident of the Baker's Wife, who, having lost her way in the
woods, falls off a cliff (a rather peculiar geographical feature
to be found in the middle of a European forest), seems even
more random and unmotivated.

The movie gets off to a rollicking start; the opening number benefits from the opportunity for cross-cutting offered

by cinema and the chance to include flashbacks to how the Baker's father stole the beans and the Witch was punished with ugliness. It also showcases Colleen Atwood's delightful, often dazzling costumes and the carefully chosen cast. Lapine cleverly adds an explanation for the Witch's deadline of a mere three days to retrieve the magic objects: a blue moon will appear on the third day, a rare natural occurrence that allows for some very pretty computer-generated images.

Yet, soon after the opening it becomes apparent that Rob Marshall seems at a loss as to how to stage some of the songs, partly because they usually interrupt the action in order to tell us what the characters have just learned and thus risk becoming static interludes in a movie musical. The only number in this mode that works is 'On the Steps of the Palace', because it literally stops time, with everything and everybody freezing while Cinderella makes up her mind. 'I Know Things Now' and 'Giants in the Sky' fall flat: in the first, Little Red Ridinghood appears to hold the Baker hostage, forcing him to listen while she recounts her experiences in the Wolf's stomach, which are illustrated in a style that owes a great deal to Tim Burton's *Alice in Wonderland* (2010, also financed and distributed by Disney). But why show us the girl's journey, and not what happened when Cinderella attends the ball or Jack's adventures above the clouds? And why should the Baker be interested in her new-found wisdom as he has more pressing matters to attend to? In contrast, 'Giants in the Sky' is performed with Jack clambering up a tall tree in an unsuccessful attempt to make the song more 'cinematic'; instead, in spite of a charming performance by the vivacious Daniel Huttlestone, the action here grinds to a complete halt.

'Agony' is a lot of fun, partly because the actors bring exactly the right mixture of dashing good looks and narcissistic competitiveness to it, and partly because of the perfect use of real-life locations. Without the later reprise of the song, however, the dalliance of Cinderella's Prince with the Baker's Wife no longer suggests a recurrent pattern, but becomes a rather inexplicable one-off affair.

Since the dramaturgical method of having the characters address the audience directly – an alienation effect that in turn

Figure 4.1 Stunning location work combined with performances pitched at exactly the right level of exalted ardour: Billy Magnussen (left) as Rapunzel's Prince and Chris Pine (right) as Cinderella's Prince, in the 2014 movie version of *ITW*. This scene was filmed at the artificial waterfall at Virginia Water Lake, Windsor. Photograph by AF Archive, Courtesy of Alamy Stock Foto.

prepares us for their re-appearance after they have 'died' –
is not used in the screenplay, the return of both the Baker's
father and his wife near the end is puzzling. Are these appa-
ritions? And why do the deceased only impart words of wisdom to the Baker? It would seem more urgent and thus more
logical for the dead to console the now-orphaned children
(i.e. Jack and Little Red Ridinghood), so why are they not
visited by their mother and/or grandmother?

The film runs into real trouble at the end when two ballads
('No One Is Alone' and 'Children Will Listen') follow one
after the other. Marshall's decision to illustrate the latter –
sung on the soundtrack – while the camera slowly moves
upward to allow one last look over all of fairyland, reeks of
desperation and wastes a marvellous song. Worse, it deprives
the film of a proper ending. It just stops. (When I saw the
film in the cinema, the audience was puzzled for a moment:
was that it?)

All through the film the actors with experience in stage
and film musicals (like Anna Kendrick, Christine Baranski
and Tracey Ullman) acquit themselves beautifully, and Chris
Pine and Billy Magnussen as the two princes seize their
opportunity to turn 'Agony' into a riot. What may not have
been expected, though, is that the two most quietly effective
performances are given by James Corden and Emily Blunt
as the Baker and his wife; both create characters with real
warmth and charm. Although neither of them at the time
of filming was known as a singer, they master Sondheim's
difficult score with apparent ease and excel at expressing their
characters' emotions through song.

For her turn as the Witch, Meryl Streep earned a record-
breaking nineteenth Academy Award nomination, which is
not surprising, since one cannot help noticing how much she

is acting. As usual, she gives a highly intelligent and immaculately prepared performance: her singing has never been better and every single line-reading is carefully worked out. But flamboyance does not come naturally to Streep because her greatest gift as a performer lies in how much she grounds her characters in a recognizable reality. So, instead of merely stylizing a larger-than-life personality to channel the Witch's histrionics, she performs them studiously, which for some may take the fun out of the role – what is missing is the juicy energy that a bit of camp would add to the proceedings. It also does not help that at the age of 65 Streep was too old to play a witch restored to her youthful glamour. Yet, instead of allowing Streep to look alluring as herself once she is no longer buried in prosthetics and make-up, the inexplicable decision was taken to change the actor's natural appearance. After her transformation, the Witch sports a false set of teeth that make her resemble 1940s film star, Greer Garson. She is outfitted in a stunning gown of various shades of Prussian blue – a colour scheme matched by her wig – but she does not have any wrinkles, even though she is clearly not meant to be younger than her mid-forties. With porcelain teeth and porcelain features that – like all china – provide hard surfaces, the Witch looks glazed, rather than simply restored to beauty.

In spite of the cuts to the show, the second half of the film drags as it loses narrative drive; this is when the audience is likely to notice the flaws in the movie's design and may start asking why Rapunzel's hair isn't really yellow and why Cinderella visits the Prince's ball three nights running in the same dress. This goes back to the stage version, where it undoubtedly helped to rein in the costume budget; it represents one of many details that James Lapine clearly did not feel necessary to question when he adapted his own libretto for the screen. But her appearances in the ball transpire differently in the original fairy tale, which sees the girl wearing a new gown every night – each more resplendent than the one before – and it seems rather niggardly to omit this considering the film's reported budget of $50 million, which should have allowed for more variety.

Even though the Giant's appearance provides an opportunity for many special effects shots and her defeat is turned into a scene of suspense, the fight against her lacks urgency. It needs to be pointed out here that the Giant's death happens off-stage in the original not just because of budgetary constraints and the limitations of what can be done in the theatre. Keeping her death mostly out of sight allows the musical to focus on the moral dilemma leading to the attack, highlighting the ethical convictions motivating the action.

Perhaps the movie's biggest problem is that it fails to navigate convincingly from enchantment to darkness. The woods are never really frightening, partly because the location work and the studio sets only match up to a certain degree. Dion Beebe's careful lighting, with the dappled sun- or moonlight streaming through the forest leaves, is often merely pretty instead of dangerously alluring. The screen version never manages to shake off the shackles of the Disney brand of entertainment for all age groups. When it was announced that the Walt Disney Corporation would finance a movie version of *ITW*, there were immediate concerns that the company's reputation for wholesome family entertainment could result in a screen adaptation that would downplay the grim elements of the stage show; the final result confirmed these suspicions. All of the violence and several of the deaths occur off-screen, which prompts

the question as to why insist on their inclusion in the storyline if the movie is then unwilling to give them their due
by allowing them screen time? Brutal punishments and
death are part of many a fairy tale, but the film adaptation
of *ITW* incorporates them so off-handedly and arbitrarily
that they seem unnecessary irritations, unwarranted by the
plot, which mainly serve to undercut the audience's enjoyment of what often resembles a traditional Disney family
film. For instance, the manslaughter of Jack's Mother is
reduced to an accident: the Steward simply pushes her to
the ground instead of hitting her over the head. This scene
is so confusingly staged that it comes as a genuine surprise
to the audience that she actually has died. In the end, the
film adaptation dilutes what made the stage show so unique
among fairy tale musicals, but does not go so far as to completely reconceive the material in the mould of other Disney fairy tales. The result is a curious oddity that teeters
uneasily between traditionally upbeat cartoon musicals (in
numbers like the title song and 'Agony') and fantasy fare
like the later *Harry Potter* films or *Pan's Labyrinth* (2006),
which were aimed at older or even adult audiences, without
fully satisfying the core fans of either genre.

The film adaptation was a substantial hit, earning $213
million worldwide and thus outgrossing Tim Burton's adaptation of *Sweeney Todd* (global box office: $152 million).
The popularity of its cast members, especially Streep and
Kendrick, and the fact that it is now part of the Disney trea-
sure chest of fairy tale adaptations will ensure that the movie
remains in the public eye for years to come. But although it
was financially successful, the film's mixed reception – both
by critics (its Rotten Tomatoes and Metacritic scores are
71 per cent and 69 per cent, respectively) and public (its

average rating on www.amazon.com is 3.3 out of 5 stars, very low for a Disney release) – left no doubt that the combination of the wholesome Disney brand and Sondheim's very own brand of intellectual playfulness which offers no moral certainties, was a shotgun wedding at best. Still, while it may not succeed as a whole, when the film does work, especially during some of its earlier stretches, the adaption rises to the occasion – even if this amounts to merely a few 'Moments in the Woods'.

Conclusion *or* 'Be ready for the journey'

To some degree, *Into the Woods* mirrors how one's relationship with fairy tales changes over time: we may first encounter them when we are children as enchanting clear-cut narratives of heroism triumphing over villainy. But, as we grow older, we realize that life is too complex to be reduced to simple good vs evil scenarios, and at the point we abandon them and turn towards more challenging reading material as a more apt guide to the society we live in. In a similar way the musical with its increasingly murky moral landscape progressively replaces the primary colours of children's stories with swaths of grey and thus moves from child-appropriate fun and simplicity to more grown-up concerns of communal responsibility and dealing with loss. Similar to the readers of fairy tales, the show's characters thus learn on their journey through the woods that the original 'happily ever after' has a limited 'use-by' date before it is revealed as a lie we tell ourselves and our children to make their environment seem less frightening. Yet, the musical never loses sight of the fact that it is fairy tales that first feed our hunger for stories and that they are an important stepping stone on our way to discovering more complex artistic expressions of the world we live in. They are the starting point for our journey into wider society and into the realm of literature and related arts; they also provide the foundation for our appreciation of the craft of story-telling, a craft that is both cherished and exemplified by *ITW*.

References

Primary text

Sondheim, Stephen/Lapine, James (1989), *Into the Woods*, New York: Theatre Communications Group Inc.

Secondary sources

Anon. (2002[a]), 'Cinderella and the Prince: Happily Ever After', *The Sondheim Review* 3: 22–23.

Anon. (2002[b]), 'How the *Woods* Movie Might Have Opened', *The Sondheim Review* 3: 25.

Anon. (2002[c]), 'Peters Wanted a Chance to Learn', *The Sondheim Review* 3: 23.

Banfield, Stephen (1994), *Sondheim's Broadway Musicals*, Ann Arbor: University of Michigan Press.

Cartmell, Dan J. (1983), *Stephen Sondheim and the Concept Musical*, Ann Arbor: University Microfilms International.

Gordon, Joanne (1990), *Art Isn't Easy. The Achievement of Stephen Sondheim*, Carbondale/Edwardsville: Southern Illinois University Press.

Gottfried, Martin (1993), *Sondheim*, New York: Harry N. Abrams.

Hirsch, Foster (1989), *Harold Prince and the American Musical Theatre*, Cambridge: Cambridge University Press.

Jubin, Olaf (2005), *Entertainment in der Kritik. Eine komparative Analyse von amerikanischen, britischen und deutschsprachigen Rezensionen zu den Musicals von Stephen Sondheim und Andrew Lloyd Webber*, Herbolzheim: Centaurus.

Mankin, Nina (1988), 'The PAJ Casebook #2 *Into the Woods*', *Performing Arts Journal* 1: 46–66.

Roberts, Terri (2002), 'Gleason Recalls Her Moments in the Woods', *The Sondheim Review* 3: 20.

Savran, David (1988), 'Stephen Sondheim', in *In Their Own Words. Contemporary American Playwrights*, New York: Theatre Communications Group Inc., pp. 223–239.

Sondheim, Stephen (2011), *Look, I Made a Hat. Collected Lyrics (1981–2011), with Attendant Comments, Amplifications, Dogmas, Harangues, Digressions, Anecdotes and Miscellany*, New York: Virgin Books.

Secrest, Meryle (1998), *Stephen Sondheim. A Life*, New York: Bantam Doubleday.

Sheader, Timothy (2010), 'Notes from the Director', *Into the Woods. Programme*, London: Regent's Park Enterprises, p. 9.

Spohr, Mathias/Weihe, Richard/Siedhoff, Thomas (1994), 'Stephen Sondheim', in *Pipers Enzyklopädie des Musiktheaters. Oper, Operette, Musical, Ballett. Band 5: Werke Puccini – Spontini*, ed. by Carl Dahlhaus, Munich/Zurich: Piper, pp. 740–747.

Taylor, Millie (2009), *British Pantomime Performance*, Chicago: University of Chicago Press.

Walsh, Michael (1989), *Andrew Lloyd Webber. His Life and Works*, London/New York: Viking Press.

Young, Karen (2000), '"Every Day a Little Death". Sondheim's Un-musicalizing of Marriage', in *Reading Stephen Sondheim. A Collection of Critical Essays*, ed. by Sandor Goodhart, New York: Garland, pp. 77–88.

Zadan, Craig (1989), *Sondheim & Co*. Second, revised edition, London: Pavilion Books.

Discography

Into the Woods. Original Broadway Cast Recording (1987), Master-
 works Broadway 82876-68636-2.
Into the Woods. Original London Cast Recording (1990), RCA
 Victor RD 60 752.
Into the Woods. Broadway Revival Cast (2002), Nonesuch 7559-
 79686-2.
Into the Woods. 2-Disc Deluxe Edition Soundtrack (2014), Walt Disney
 Records 005008732164.

Filmography

Into the Woods. Original Broadway Cast (1987). DVD, Image Entertainment 8573861482.

Into the Woods. Regent's Park Open Air Theatre (2010). Digital Theatre Live Recording. Available at www.digitaltheatre.com.

Into the Woods. Film (2014). DVD, Walt Disney Studios Home Entertainment, 21A BUA0248501.

Index